Development Centre S

The Visible Hand of China in Latin America

by

Javier Santiso

OECD

DEVELOPMENT CENTRE OF THE ORGANISATION
FOR ECONOMIC CO-OPERATION AND DEVELOPMENT

ORGANISATION FOR ECONOMIC CO-OPERATION AND DEVELOPMENT

The OECD is a unique forum where the governments of 30 democracies work together to address the economic, social and environmental challenges of globalisation. The OECD is also at the forefront of efforts to understand and to help governments respond to new developments and concerns, such as corporate governance, the information economy and the challenges of an ageing population. The Organisation provides a setting where governments can compare policy experiences, seek answers to common problems, identify good practice and work to co-ordinate domestic and international policies.

The OECD member countries are: Australia, Austria, Belgium, Canada, the Czech Republic, Denmark, Finland, France, Germany, Greece, Hungary, Iceland, Ireland, Italy, Japan, Korea, Luxembourg, Mexico, the Netherlands, New Zealand, Norway, Poland, Portugal, the Slovak Republic, Spain, Sweden, Switzerland, Turkey, the United Kingdom and the United States. The Commission of the European Communities takes part in the work of the OECD.

OECD Publishing disseminates widely the results of the Organisation's statistics gathering and research on economic, social and environmental issues, as well as the conventions, guidelines and standards agreed by its members.

© OECD 2007

No reproduction, copy, transmission or translation of this publication may be made without written permission. Applications should be sent to OECD Publishing rights@oecd.org or by fax 33 1 45 24 99 30. Permission to photocopy a portion of this work should be addressed to the Centre français d'exploitation du droit de copie (CFC), 20, rue des Grands-Augustins, 75006 Paris, France, fax 33 1 46 34 67 19, contact@cfcopies.com or (for US only) to Copyright Clearance Center (CCC), 222 Rosewood Drive Danvers, MA 01923, USA, fax 1 978 646 8600, info@copyright.com.

THE DEVELOPMENT CENTRE

The Development Centre of the Organisation for Economic Co-operation and Development was established by decision of the OECD Council on 23 October 1962 and comprises 22 member countries of the OECD: Austria, Belgium, the Czech Republic, Finland, France, Germany, Greece, Iceland, Ireland, Italy, Korea, Luxembourg, Mexico, the Netherlands, Norway, Portugal, Slovak Republic, Spain, Sweden, Switzerland, Turkey and the United Kingdom as well as Brazil since March 1994, Chile since November 1998, India since February 2001, Romania since October 2004, Thailand since March 2005 and South Africa since May 2006. The Commission of the European Communities also takes part in the Centre's Governing Board.

The Development Centre, whose membership is open to both OECD and non-OECD countries, occupies a unique place within the OECD and in the international community. Members finance the Centre and serve on its Governing Board, which sets the biennial work programme and oversees its implementation.

The Centre links OECD members with developing and emerging economies and fosters debate and discussion to seek creative policy solutions to emerging global issues and development challenges. Participants in Centre events are invited in their personal capacity.

A small core of staff works with experts and institutions from the OECD and partner countries to fulfil the Centre's work programme. The results are discussed in informal expert and policy dialogue meetings, and are published in a range of high-quality products for the research and policy communities. The Centre's *Study Series* presents in-depth analyses of major development issues. *Policy Briefs* and *Policy Insights* summarise major conclusions for policy makers; *Working Papers* deal with the more technical aspects of the Centre's work.

For an overview of the Centre's activities, please see **www.oecd.org/dev**

THE OPINIONS EXPRESSED AND ARGUMENTS EMPLOYED IN DEVELOPMENT CENTRE PUBLICATIONS ARE THE SOLE RESPONSIBILITY OF THE AUTHOR AND DO NOT NECESSARILY REFLECT THOSE OF THE OECD, ITS DEVELOPMENT CENTRE OR OF THE GOVERNMENTS OF THEIR MEMBER COUNTRIES.

ISBN: 9789264027961

Foreword

This publication is part of the Development Centre's work leading to its Flagship publication, the Latin American Economic Outlook, as defined under the 2007/08 work programme.

Table of Contents

Foreword 4

Acknowledgements 6

Preface 7

Introduction 9

Chapter 1   Should Latin America Fear China?
       by Eduardo Lora 15

Chapter 2   Angel or Devil? China's Trade Impact on Latin American Emerging Markets
       by Jorge Blázquez-Lidoy, Javier Rodríguez and Javier Santiso 45

Chapter 3   China and Latin America: Trade Competition, 1990-2002
       by Sanjaya Lall and John Weiss 85

Chapter 4   Competing with the Dragon: Latin American and Chinese Exports to the US Market
       by Ernesto López-Córdova, Alejandro Micco and Danielken Molina 109

Chapter 5   Does China Have an Impact on Foreign Direct Investment to Latin America?
       by Alicia Garcia-Herrero and Daniel Santabárbera 133

ISBN: 9789264027961

Acknowledgements

The Development Centre would like to thank participants in its March 2006 "Asian Drivers" conference for their valuable insights and comments on many of the issues raised in this volume.

Drafts and different elements of the book were presented in meetings and conferences held at Georgetown University, (October 2004), Columbia University (October 2004), The World Bank (October 2004, May 2005 and June 2006), LACEA (November 2004), CAF (November 2004), OECD Development Centre (January 2005), IDB (April 2005), Casa América in Madrid (June 2006), Swiss Latin American Chamber of Commerce in Zurich (June 2006), Standard Chartered in London (June 2006), Suez Group in Paris (September 2006), Exane BNP Paribas in Geneva (September 2006), French Ministry of Foreign Affairs (October 2006) and the European Commission in Brussels (November 2006). The authors and editors also extend their appreciation to participants in these events whose comments represented valuable contributions to the final form of the book. Finally, former Deputy Secretary General of the OECD Robert Cornell is to be thanked for his excellent editing of the volume.

This study was made possible by the generous support of the Spanish Ministries of Finance and Economy and of Foreign Affairs for activities at the OECD Development Centre related to Latin America.

Preface

This detailed study of the impact of China on Latin America is part of a major Development Centre initiative that culminated in a March 2006 conference. The event brought together experts from OECD and non-OECD countries to discuss the impacts of the Asian Drivers on other developing economies in Africa, Asia and Latin America.

China has been a powerful global player in the past, as detailed by Angus Maddison in earlier work for the OECD Development Centre[1], contributing as much as nearly a third of world GDP as late as the beginning of the 19th century. Its recovery over the past decade has been spectacular, creating both opportunities and challenges for many other countries, most notably developing countries and emerging economies. For Latin America, China looks more like a "trade angel", as it provides an outlet for commodities from the region. China's trade impact on Latin America is, thus, positive; directly, through a boom of exports, and indirectly, through better terms of trade.

The rise of China is also a challenge for Latin American countries. If they are to keep building on their comparative advantage, reforms must continue, particularly in the area of infrastructure.

The following chapters present detailed evidence of the positive and negative trade and financial impacts of the rise of China on Latin America, demonstrating that this is probably one of the regions in the world to benefit most. Some of the authors concentrate their analysis on the trade impacts while others deal with foreign direct investment. All of them note that China represents

---

1. See, OECD Development Centre Studies:

   MADDISON, A. (2003), *The World Economy: Historical Statistics*, Paris.

   MADDISON, A. (2001), *The World Economy: A Millennial Perspective*, Paris.

   MADDISON, A. (1998), *Chinese Economic Performance in the Long Run*, Paris.

a unique opportunity for Latin America to build on the traditional endowments of the region. The major policy issue will be how to continue to capitalise on the Chinese windfall while avoiding the risk of being pushed into a raw materials corner, instead of deepening integration into the global value chain.

Beyond trade, what is also emerging is a notable shift in global patterns of economic interdependence. Economic ties between Latin America and Asia were already strong, especially with Japan and Korea. The emergence of China – and India – extends and deepens dramatically these ties. Latin America is looking more and more towards Asia; emerging Asia seeks resources and new markets in Latin Ameria. For Europe and the United States, this is also a wake-up call.

Louka T. Katseli
Director, OECD Development Centre
March 2007

Introduction

China: A Helping Hand for Latin America?

by Javier Santiso

China's economic boom represents a major global change. Over the last few years, China has expanded by leaps and bounds and become both a threat to and an opportunity for emerging markets. Its growing demand for raw materials is at the same time a bonanza and a challenge for developing countries.

The Chinese boom brings a positive windfall boosting trade exports of countries whose endowments are commodity related. This appetite for raw materials is, however, also contributing to nominal and real exchange rate appreciations in most Latin American countries leading to lower competitiveness in manufacturing sectors. At the same time, China has emerged as a major exporter at both the labour-intensive, low technology and, increasingly, at the knowledge-intensive, higher technology end of the product spectrum. It is presenting challenges to most developing countries, and particularly other global trade champions like Mexico in nearly all sectors, from textiles to most industrial products with higher value-added.

Should Latin America fear the emergence of this new global economic player? This question is the basis of Eduardo Lora's Chapter 1, which compares the respective strengths of the Chinese economy relative to Latin America; these or such strengths include size, macroeconomic stability, abundant low-cost labour, rapidly expanding physical infrastructure, ability to innovate and massive ratios of investments and savings. This is also the central question posed by all other contributing experts and scholars from leading international institutions and academia, including the Inter-American Development Bank, the Asian Development Bank, the OECD Development Centre, the Central Bank of Spain, the Central Bank of Chile, Oxford University, and private banks such as BBVA (Banco Bilbao Vizcaya Argentaria), one of the leading European banks that is also the major financial player in Latin America.

China's trade impact on Latin America is mostly positive, both directly, through an export boom, and indirectly, through better terms of trade. China looks like a "trade angel" and a "helping hand" as well as being an outlet for commodities from the region. With galloping GDP growth and a scarcity of arable land, China's appetite for natural resources and farm products seems good news for Latin America. With $50 billion worth of trade and investments in Latin America in 2005, China is already a major partner.

To analyse China's trade impact on the rest of the world, Blázquez, Rodríguez and Santiso look at the export and import structure of the country in Chapter 2. They use a database of 620 different goods and build two indexes of trade competition in the US market in order to compare the Chinese impact over the period 1998-2004 on 34 different economies, of which 15 are in Latin America. This shows that Venezuela, Bolivia and Chile are those with the lowest indexes among the 34 and thus, those that suffer least from Chinese trade competition. Brazil, Colombia and Peru are in an intermediate position. The countries that are most exposed to Chinese competition in the United States are Central American countries and Mexico.

Sanjaya Lall and John Weiss reach similar conclusions in Chapter 3, which analyses and compares China's and Latin America's export performance and specialisation patterns in the world as a whole, including the United States, the main market for both. They show that the trade structure of most Latin American countries is generally more complementary than competitive with China's. Lall and Weiss join the earlier authors, however, in underlining the point that if China represents a unique trade opportunity for Latin America, it may nonetheless pose a serious threat to its long-term development: heavy reliance on resource-based products is not conducive to technological upgrading and diversification. A potential revaluation of the *renmimbi* could enhance competitiveness of Latin American products in US markets, as stressed by López-Córdova *et al.* in Chapter 4. This issue is likely to remain a major structural challenge.

China's emergence is a wake-up call for Latin America. Countries like Mexico will have to boost reforms in order to remain in the competitiveness race. Labour costs will clearly no longer offer a competitive advantage, at least in the medium term. A better way to deal with the Chinese challenge will be to push ahead the agenda of reforms, particularly in the area of infrastructures.

For Mexico and Central America, proximity to the United States is a major strategic asset on which to capitalise. The best way of doing this is to improve the efficiency of roads, ports, railways and airports in order to lower transaction and transportation costs.

For other Latin American countries, China is likely to remain a trade angel. Not surprisingly, the countries that mainly export raw materials face lower competition. This is only to be expected, bearing in mind that China is a net importer of such commodities. In 2003, Chinese imports of nickel doubled, its copper imports grew by 15 per cent, oil by 30 per cent and soy beans by 70 per cent. China has become the world's leading consumer of copper, zinc, platinum, iron and steel.

Most Latin American countries are thus witnessing a tremendous increase in their exports. The region's commodity-specialising exporters are well able to fulfil the needs of growing Chinese demand contributing 47 per cent of world exports of soy beans and 40 per cent of world exports of copper. Latin American exports towards China jumped by impressive numbers in nominal terms. From 2000 to 2003, Brazil's exports increased by 500 per cent, Argentina's by 360 per cent and Chile's by 240 per cent. Even Mexico, a global trader in manufactures, saw its exports towards China increasing by 1000 per cent over the period.

China has become Brazil's second and fastest-growing export market but these exports are concentrated on five commodities that account for 75 per cent of Brazil's exports to China. Soy beans are the major commodity exported towards China, both for Brazil and Argentina. For Chile and Peru, the bulk of exports towards China are concentrated on a single commodity, namely copper.

Despite concentration in a small basket of commodities, China's strong demand for raw materials is, nevertheless, good news for Latin America. From 2000 to 2005, China represented nearly 40 per cent of the total growth in world oil demand. China's growing thirst for oil has been driving oil prices up and boosting trade surpluses of oil exporters such as Venezuela, Ecuador and Colombia. The surge of Chinese imports of copper over the last few years also caused prices to rise and has been a boost for Chile and Peru, two other economies that have registered record trade surpluses in 2004 and 2005.

China is not only a major trade partner for Latin America. During the coming decade, it might well offer a helping and visible hand in terms of capital flows. China does not seem to compete with Latin America for foreign direct investment. It attracted as much FDI as the whole of Latin America over the past years, but this does not seem to have been at the expense of Latin American countries. As underlined by Alicia García-Herrero and Daniel

Santabárbara in Chapter 5, there is no substitution from Latin American inward FDI to China for the period analysed, namely from 1984 to 2001. However, when assessing the impact country by country and for the more recent period 1995-2001, the picture changes a little as China's inward FDI appears to have hampered that of some countries in the region, namely Mexico and Colombia.

In fact, instead of fearing increasing competition from China for capturing FDI, Latin America may once again be well placed to attract Chinese interests. The region has a surplus commodity endowment that boosts synergies with China's need and strategy to secure food and energy imports in order to avoid shortages. Chinese investments can and will be channelled not only in agribusiness and commodity-related industries but also in infrastructures, roads and ports.

In 2003, China's outward investment more than doubled in the course of a year (although it is still at a low level) and Latin America received one third of world Chinese FDI. The following year, nearly 50 per cent of Chinese FDI went to Latin America (16 per cent in 2005, of a total record of 7 billion of dollars invested overseas). The need to secure food and commodities is boosting FDI through strategic international partnerships. In Mexico, China is already setting up manufacturing companies and Chinese interests in Argentina's railway construction or agribusiness-related projects are also on the rise. Some of the biggest investments carried out abroad by Chinese companies are already located in Latin America, namely in Brazil in the steel and iron industry. In 2004, The Chinese state oil company Sinopec invested $1 billion in a joint venture with Petrobras for the construction of a gas pipeline linking south to northeast Brazil. Other deals the Chinese have recently signed included iron ore shipments from Companhia Vale do Rio Doce (CVRD), one of the world's largest mining concerns, for Shanghai's famous Baoshan Steel Mill. In 2005, Codelco, the Chilean copper giant signed an historic trade contract with Chinese Minmetals.

It is not only Chinese companies that are interested in coming to Latin America; Brazilian ones for example are also looking to opportunities in China, the most active being companies like jet maker Embraer or Marcopolo, Brazil's and South America's largest bus producer. While there are only 15 Brazilian companies active in China, there are already 4 000 from Canada.

It is clear that Latin America is looking towards China and Asia — and this is reciprocal (Santiso, 2005*a*). This is a major shift: for the first time in its history Latin America can benefit from not one but three major world engines of growth. Until the 1980s, the United States was the major trade partner of the region. During the 1990s, the boom in European investments provided a second engine of growth. Today, in this new decade and century, the emergence of China, and above all Asia, is proving to be a third engine of growth for Latin America. The Asian demand for commodities offers Latin America a unique historic opportunity but for that the region will have to do more than simply surfing the wave.

Even for those Latin American surfers that are benefiting from the Chinese windfall, the major policy issue will be not only to capitalise on this *bonanza* but above all to avoid the risk of being pushed into a raw materials corner and to remain integrated into the value chain of global production.

Beyond the trade and financial impacts of China on Latin America, there might be a more subtle effect that could be labelled a "cognitive impact". China symbolises a success story, catching the attention of development economists, policy makers and firm managers in both developed and developing countries. If the Chinese success story is striking, it is because this development trajectory testifies to the impressive economic pragmatism of China's policy makers who apply marketfriendly policies, driven by the state, to promote reforms and productive restructuring. This capitalist *bricolage* is unique, even if it is similar to previous Asian experiences, notably those of Japan, Singapore or Malaysia. What remains different is that in the case of China it is driven by a Communist Party.

The political economy of pragmatism is more prevalent today around the world than was the case a few years ago. Without any reference to a macro paradigm or a text-book model, China pushed ahead with its own trajectory. There were no "Chicago Boys", or "Money Doctors" landing in Beijing to advise what to do or not to do. In Latin America, this pragmatism has also been at work in countries like Chile, Mexico and Brazil (Santiso, 2006). All in all, these experiences, though each very different and unique, are pointing to the fact that there is no magic formula or magic key that opens the box of development.

Bibliography

Devlin, R., A. Estevadeordal and A. Rodríguez (2006) (eds.), *The Emergence of China: Opportunities and Challenges for Latin America and the Caribbean*, Harvard University Press, David Rockefeller Centre and Inter-American Development Bank; Cambridge, Mass.

Santiso, J. (2006), *Latin America's Political Economy of the Possible. Beyond Good Revolutionaries and Free-Marketeers*, MIT Press, Cambridge, Mass.

Santiso, J. (2005*a*), "La emergencia de China y su impacto en América Latina", *Economía Exterior*, Vol. 19, 107, September-October, pp. 97-111.

Santiso, J. (2005*b*), "América Latina y Asia: bailando con los tigres y los dragones asiáticos", *in* C. Malamud and P. Isbell (eds.), *El Anuario Elcano: América Latina 2004-2005*, Instituto Real Elcano and Ariel, Madrid, pp. 275-298.

Chapter 1

Should Latin America Fear China?

by Eduardo Lora[1]

> **Abstract**[2]
>
> This chapter compares growth conditions in China and Latin America to assess fears that China will displace Latin America in the coming decades. China's strengths include the size of the economy, macroeconomic stability, abundant low-cost labour, the rapid expansion of physical infrastructure and the ability to innovate. Its weaknesses stem from insufficient separation between market and state. They involve poor corporate governance, a fragile financial system and misallocation of savings. Both regions also share important weaknesses. The rule of law is weak, corruption is endemic and education is both poor and very poorly distributed.

Introduction

China has been the world's fastest-growing economy for the last three decades. Since economic reforms started in 1978, the economy has shown average real growth of 9.4 per cent per year. Eliminating the most obvious factors of overestimation that the official statistics may contain, Alwyn Young (2003) has estimated this growth as 1.7 percentage points lower, with annual per capita income growth at 6.1 per cent instead of the officially reported 7.8 per cent[3]. Even with Chinese growth rates two or three points lower than officially reported, however, Latin America does not shine in comparison. Its average annual growth rate since 1978 has been only 2.3 per cent. While per capita income in China increased more than sevenfold between 1978 and 2005 according to official figures (or fourfold with Young's adjustments), Latin America reported an average increase of only 20 per cent. While manufacturing has led in China with average growth rates of over 12 per cent, the performance of the Latin American manufacturing sector has been disappointing too; its annual average growth was only 0.3 per cent in the 1980s and 2.5 per cent in the 1990s[4].

Since China joined the World Trade Organisation in December 2001, these divergences have attracted growing attention because of fears that competition from Chinese products was having a devastating effect on clothing *maquilas*, electronics products industries and many other industrial products from thousands of companies around Latin America. Competition from China may be one reason for the decline in foreign direct investment (FDI) to Latin America (Figure 1.1)[5] [for a discussion see Chapter 5 in this book]. Mexico's FDI inflows fell from $26.6 billion in 2001 to $11 billion in 2003, and 960 firms left the country with an estimated loss of over 300 000 jobs (254 000 in the *maquilas* alone)[6]. Although these trends partly reversed in 2004, as FDI rose to $14.4 billion with an estimated increase of 70 000 *maquiladora* jobs, fears mounted again when FDI fell back to $11.3 billion in 2005. For Latin America as a whole, although FDI climbed from a low of $32.6 billion in 2003 to $47.3 billion in 2005, it remains substantially below its 1999 peak of $79.3 billion[7].

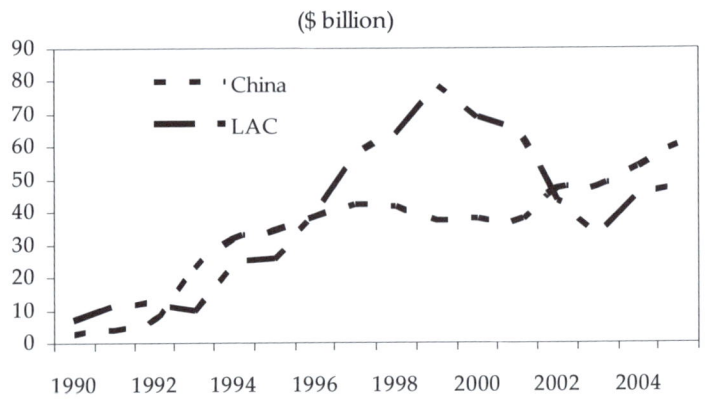

Figure 1.1. **Net Foreign Direct Investment**
($ billion)

Source: CEPAL (various years) for Latin America and the Caribbean (LAC) and World Bank (various years), the Economist (2005) and International Monetary Fund, IMF (various years) for China.

This chapter attempts to assess whether fears that China will displace Latin America in the coming decades are well grounded. Several studies have tackled this issue from a microeconomic perspective, comparing factor endowments, export structures or key cost components such as labour or transportation costs[8]. This one takes a different approach. It compares China and Latin America in terms of growth performance as well as their ability to attract foreign direct investment. While this approach does not lend itself to empirical testing, it provides a more comprehensive and balanced view of China's economy, which may be useful both to prospective investors and to practitioners and analysts, especially those already familiar with Latin America.

The chapter argues that China's strengths relative to Latin America derive from the size of the economy, its macroeconomic stability, the abundance of low-cost labour, the rapid expansion of its physical infrastructure and its ability to innovate. China's main weaknesses are by-products of the lack of separation between market and state. This results in poor corporate governance, a fragile financial system and a tendency to misallocate savings, currently manifested through excess investment in many sectors. China also shares several deep deficiencies with Latin America. In both regions, the rule of law is weak, corruption is endemic and education is poor and very poorly distributed. Broadly based innovation is discouraged by the lack of respect for property rights and by norms and practices that inhibit competition. In the medium term, both China's and Latin America's ability to correct their institutional flaws will determine their capacity to achieve higher income levels and fully to integrate into the world economy.

China's Strengths

Countries do not compete, but companies compete, as Paul Krugman (1994) cautions. China's growth does not occur at the expense of Latin America's, even if some foreign investors have preferred to go to China. In fact, Chinese growth has most certainly been favourable to Latin America, simply because China is the most powerful source of world economic growth. Since 2000, China's contribution to global GDP growth (in purchasing-power-parity terms) has been bigger than that of the United States, and more than half as big as the combined contribution of India, Brazil and Russia, the three next-largest emerging economies (*The Economist*, 23 March 2006). This results in expanded markets and better export prices, especially for primary goods, which are a very important source of external revenue for Latin America. It also results in higher world savings, which help to finance countries with external deficits, as is usually the case for Latin American countries and the United States. The enormous US current-account deficit, which benefits Latin America, can be sustained only by direct external financing from China and other Asian countries. Consequently, underscoring China's strengths in relation to Latin America is useful for understanding why China is more successful, but it does not mean that conditions in Latin America would be better if China lacked these strengths.

Size

China is the sixth largest economy in the world. At the growth rates it has enjoyed in recent decades it appears set to become the largest in less than 40 years, based on GDP valued at market exchange rates. With GDP valued at PPP rates, however, it already is the world's second largest economy; it will overtake the United States in less than a decade if both countries maintain their current growth rates. China also has an impressive importance in world trade, because it is more open than other countries, more notably India, Brazil and the United States. These countries' exports and imports are no more than 25 per cent of GDP, while China's trade represents half of its GDP at market value[9].

Size generates advantages because it helps attract foreign investment to exploit the domestic market and produce for export, tapping the enormous supply of labour that is China's most abundant resource[10]. In such a huge economy, companies can exploit economies of scale in production, transport and marketing that are decisive for penetrating international markets (Hummels, 2004). The large Chinese cities also offer opportunities to exploit economies of agglomeration, facilitating the formation of company clusters that complement and compete with each other. This factor is crucial for developing and exploiting skilled labour resources and expanding sectors that depend on knowledge and innovation. In China, however, other factors — such as the special status of state companies and the poor innovation climate — prevent companies from fully using these advantages.

Sustained Growth

The best-known international competitiveness indicator is the Growth Competitiveness Index published annually by the World Economic Forum. Its latest edition ranks China 54th among 125 countries (World Economic

Forum, 2006) This does not seem very exceptional, but it is 23 places higher than that of the median Latin American country. Because of its construction method, the index tends to relate closely to countries' income levels, which means that richer countries always tend to occupy higher positions. After controlling for income, however, China occupies an extraordinary relative position. In Latin America, only Chile holds a place significantly higher than that predicted by its income level. Countries that have such good positions tend to grow more rapidly later — and conversely for countries with poor positions[11]. The indicator thus provides a good barometer of the quality of the environment for the future development of productive activity, because it incorporates factors crucial for economic growth, such as macroeconomic stability, the quality of institutions and the environment for technological improvements and innovation.

China's stable macroeconomic environment makes it stand out in comparison with Latin America. China ranks 6th according to this indicator, outperforming the typical developing country. The typical Latin American country ranks 77th, revealing that Latin America is the region with one of the world's most severe macroeconomic instability, only second to Africa. As is discussed below, the quality of China's institutions and its environment for innovation leave much to be desired, although they correspond to what is expected for China's income level.

Underlying the positive macroeconomic indicators are the level and stability of economic growth and the good risk ratings that international analysts assign to China on the basis of its growth record, low inflation rates, low levels of government debt and the soundness of its international reserves and external balance. Naturally, such measurement involves a certain amount of circularity. Because China has had rapid and stable growth in the past, it receives good risk ratings that maintain the expectation of sustained growth: this becomes a self-fulfilling prophecy. The opposite is the case for most Latin American countries. These self-fulfilling expectations, however, are a double-edged sword: although they provide time to resolve macroeconomic or structural imbalances, they also tempt countries to ignore them. This could be the case for the Chinese financial system, addressed further below. It also applies to the repressed appreciation of the renminbi, whereby an excess supply of foreign exchange has given rise to a gargantuan accumulation of international reserves. In 2005 alone, China's international reserves increased by $209 billion, reaching nearly $819 billion (or 42.8 per cent of GDP at current prices)[12]. This represents a "war chest" that, along with other features of the Chinese economy, offers protection against the risks of a sudden stop in capital flows and other external sector risks. Nevertheless, high reserves exert pressure on the money supply[13] and on the prices of key assets such as real estate and may eventually lead to inflation. What seems to have prevented inflation so far is the combination of fast income growth (which boosts money demand) and rapid productivity increases (which mitigate the effect of input cost increases on final prices).

Cheap and Abundant Manpower

A large domestic market and abundant cheap labour is China's most evident advantage in attracting foreign investment and exporting manufactures. The average wage in manufacturing was only $141 a month in 2004[14], lower than the current minimum wage in most Latin American countries (Figure 1.2). In 1990, the average wage was $36 a month, implying a 10.2 per cent average annual nominal increase between 1990-2004. This does not differ substantially from the economic growth rate of the period (9.7 per cent) or the growth rate of workers' productivity in the overall economy (8.5 per cent).

That industrial wages have risen at the rate of economic growth does not imply restrictions on the total labour supply. According to official sources[15], the working-age population totalled 897 million in 2003, 85 per cent of which effectively participated in the labour market. This is one of the highest rates in the world, possibly thanks to the level of participation of women in the labour market and the low fertility rates promoted by the communist system. Although employment in the overall economy has grown by only 2.5 per cent annually since 1980 (and by only 1.1 per cent since 1990), the most dynamic sectors have not suffered from labour shortages because there is redundant labour in agriculture and the state companies. Employment outside these two sectors grew at 7.9 per cent annually in 1980-2001 and at 5.3 per cent in 1990-2001 (Brooks and Tao, 2003). This process is far from exhausted. The inefficient sectors have an estimated 160 million surplus workers, and in the next quarter century the rural population could decline by 300 million people (Wolf, 2003).

Despite its importance, a multitude of restrictions that are only gradually being relaxed, constrain rural-urban migration. The most important traditional constraint is the system of household registration (*hukou*), which is required in order to remain in the cities and have access to jobs and basic services of education, healthcare and social security[16]. Migration has also been limited by emigrants' fear of losing land ownership rights in their rural areas of origin and by the stricter limit on the permitted number of births per household imposed on city residents. Since 2001, people with stable employment and

Should Latin America Fear China?

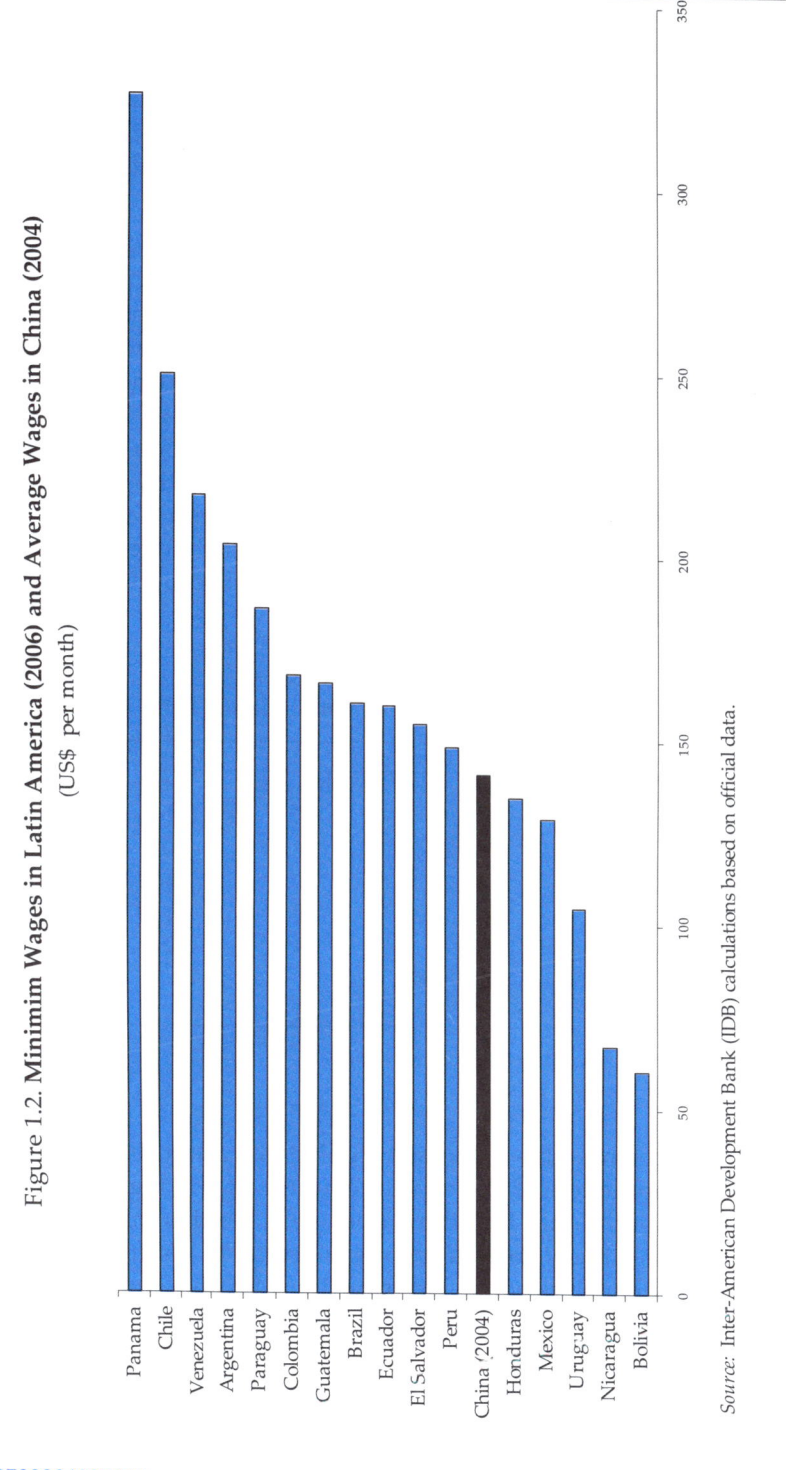

Figure 1.2. **Minimim Wages in Latin America (2006) and Average Wages in China (2004)**
(US$ per month)

Panama	~330
Chile	~252
Venezuela	~220
Argentina	~205
Paraguay	~188
Colombia	~170
Guatemala	~168
Brazil	~163
Ecuador	~162
El Salvador	~155
Peru	~148
China (2004)	~140
Honduras	~133
Mexico	~128
Uruguay	~105
Nicaragua	~65
Bolivia	~58

Source: Inter-American Development Bank (IDB) calculations based on official data.

residents have been extended permission to register in over 20 000 small towns and cities without fear of losing land rights. Several taxes on migrants have been dismantled. Severe restrictions persist in most large cities however and some time will pass before the 2001 reform is fully applied even in smaller cities (Brooks and Tao, 2003).

The movement of labour into more efficient sectors has been the major source of total factor productivity (TFP) increases, which have contributed around 3 per cent per year to GDP growth over the past two decades (Table 1.1). Based on the differences in average labour productivity between agriculture, manufacturing and the service sector, the OECD has calculated that about one quarter of the increase in productivity (and one fifth of the change in income per capita) since 1983 has come from the reallocation of labour. Yet its actual contribution could be higher, since the productivity of the marginal worker who leaves agriculture is estimated at one sixteenth that of the marginal urban worker. Although the contribution of sectoral change to GDP growth weakened in the second half of the 1990s, it has picked up since 2000 and is certainly far from finished (OECD, 2005).

Table 1.1. **Sources of Output Growth in China and Latin America**

	China		Latin America	
	1983-1993	1993-2003	1980-1990	1990-2000
GDP growth	10.5	8.9	1.3	3.3
Capital contribution	4.8	5.2	0.9	1.2
Empoyment contribution	1.3	0.3	1.8	1.7
Education contribution	1.0	1.0	1.3	1.0
Total factor productivity (residual)	3.6	2.4	-2.7	-0.6
of which:				
Sectoral change	1.5	0.1	…	…

Sources: For China, OECD (2005), and for Latin America, IDB (2001).

Latin America has also witnessed significant rural-urban migration. In 1980, half the population of the typical country of the region lived in the countryside; currently only one third does so[17]. Yet this migration has not resulted in appreciable increases in productivity. In contrast with China, productivity has had a *negative* contribution to Latin American growth, especially in the 1980s, but also more recently. The most important exception is Chile, where it has added 1.8 percentage points to average growth in the last 20 years (Loayza *et al.*, 2002)[18]. The shift of employment from country to city has not helped much because of the modest rural-urban labour-productivity gap (typically 30 per cent, see IDB, 1998) and because the sectors with the highest productivity in the cities have generated few jobs. As a result, Latin America, unlike China, has not succeeded in using the surplus labour from its inefficient sectors.

One of the reasons for this difference, although clearly not the only one, is the extremely protectionist nature of Latin American labour legislation in comparison with China's or, more accurately, with that in China's dynamic sectors. Latin America regulates in considerable detail the length of the working day as well as vacations and other worker benefits. Laws further govern conditions for the dismissal of workers and the compensation (typically fairly high) that employers must pay when they cannot demonstrate compliance with them. China has no similar national labour code. The traditional "iron rice bowl" system made state companies responsible for the obligations of labour protection and social security, which they independently granted to their workers as a mechanism for maintaining discipline in exchange for life-long job security. These benefits were very generous in other respects too, and they remain an unresolved problem for many companies. This traditional system has led to demands for improvements in pay, non-wage benefits and hiring and dismissal conditions, which vary from region to region and are partly negotiable between private companies and the local authorities and/or the labour unions. Consequently, current labour legislation for private companies provides less protection of employment conditions and job security than typical laws in Latin America, and its application is also much less predictable (OECD, 2003).

Although China has an enormous reserve of rural labour that could sustain growth during the coming decades, the longer-term prospect is hardly encouraging because of the demographic trends stemming from the one-child policy. For every person over 60 years of age, there are currently some six of working age. This ratio has held for more or less half a century, but it is beginning to fall. By 2040, China will have only two working-age people for every person over 60. Latin America starts from a younger demographic base, so that until 2040 it will keep the six-to-one ratio that China now enjoys (United Nations, 2002). China will then confront an enormous social burden that will require it to raise taxes quite far above the levels typical of Latin America.

The Physical Infrastructure Boom

Until 20 years ago China's transport, communications and energy infrastructure was very much below the standard of Latin America's most developed countries. Although serious deficiencies persist and it is difficult to meet the fast-growing demand for infrastructure services of all kinds, recent improvements have been truly noteworthy, especially in roads, ports, telecommunications and electricity, which will likely contribute to sustaining growth. Because of the privatisation process, many Latin American countries have also made good progress, although concentrated largely in the areas of telecommunications and, to a lesser extent, electricity and ports. In China, investment in infrastructure has grown much faster than the economy as a whole (rising from 2-3 per cent of GDP in the early eighties to around 9 per cent in 1998-2002). This has not been the case in Latin America, where investment in areas that have not attracted private sector attention has been neglected. Total (public and private) spending in infrastructure in Latin America is currently less than 2 per cent of its GDP, down from 3.7 per cent during 1980-85.

China's railways, the backbone of the transport system, have received large investments in recent years, including a second line from Beijing to Kowloon (Hong Kong, China) and the extension of the network to distant areas such as Kashgar in Xinjiang and to Tibet. The total length of railways in operation reached 61 000 km in 2004, up from 53 400 km in 1990. High-speed rail lines will reduce the travel time between Shanghai and Beijing from 13 hours to less than five, as part of an ambitious scheme to construct 5 400 km of high-speed rail track between 2006 and the end of the decade. Progress on roads has been even more remarkable. Since the early 1990s, inter-provincial expressways increased from zero to 34 300 km in 2004, and the total length of highways rose to 1.9 million km. Port facilities have also improved appreciably in recent years. China has 200 ports, some of them among the world's ten largest, but many are too shallow for large container ships. The most important current project is the expansion of Shanghai's port, the first phase of which was inaugurated in late 2005. The whole project will take another 15 years to complete.

China is also addressing the serious limitations facing its electricity infrastructure. The government plans to raise installed capacity from 290 GW in 2000 to 550 GW by 2010. The telecommunications sector is going through an unprecedented boom. China now has more cable television subscribers (115 million at the end of 2004) and more mobile-telephone customers

(335 million in 2004) than the United States. It also has 312 million fixed telephone lines and 94 million Internet subscribers. According to the government, the extension of the optical fibre network will bring broadband multimedia access to all urban homes by 2010 (EIU, 2006; *The Economist*, 30 March 2006).

The Ability to Innovate

With its present low level of income, China will need over two decades at current growth rates to reach half the income per capita (PPP) of the United States. A small economy in this situation would use all of that time to continue exploiting external technological development. China's size, however, imposes the need to conquer increasingly sophisticated goods markets with ever-higher technological and innovative content, and this is exactly what China has done. Supported by a massive inflow of FDI to its high-technology sectors, China has become the top provider of electronic goods. "China for the first time in 2004 surpassed America to export the most technology wares around the world, according to new figures from the Organisation for Economic Co-operation and Development. The crossover took place in 2004, when China exported $180 billion of computers, mobile phones and other digital stuff, exceeding America's international sales of $149 billion. A year earlier, in 2003, China's technology exports had overtaken those of both the European Union and Japan." (*The Economist*, 14 December 2005). The pace of innovation, as measured by the number of patents, is also picking up. China accounted for 130 000 patent applications in 2004 (the most recent year for which figures are available). That makes it number 5 globally, according to the World Intellectual Property Organization, a United Nations agency. Although China was still far behind Japan (with 450 000 patents in 2004) and the United States (with 403 000), its 2004 patent applications were six times the number in 1995.

These achievements result from a long-term, multi-pronged innovation strategy that started in the 1950s with the support of technologies deemed critical for national defence and moved in the mid-1980s to the adoption of key advanced civilian technologies. Research and development (R&D) commitments have climbed in recent years and now exceed 1 per cent of GDP (Naughton, 2004)[19]. With the important exception of Brazil, where R&D represents 0.9 per cent of GDP, R&D efforts in most Latin American countries are much smaller, at 0.2-0.6 per cent of GDP (IDB, 2001). The Chinese government has long recognised that planners do not have the technical capabilities to evaluate new technology, and it has therefore encouraged research institutions to commercialise their research products. Industrial policies also support innovation in software and integrated circuits with research funding, preferential procurement policies and tax exemptions. Crucially, both foreign-invested and domestic firms enjoy preferences. Policies generally apply across the board, with no attempt to "pick winners". Research incentives seem to have paid off handsomely. According to a 2000 R&D survey, enterprises now make some 60 per cent of China's R&D outlays. The creation of Chinese technology standards as opposed to global ones recently has further encouraged innovation. This gives Chinese firms a competitive advantage, because it delays the entry of foreign technology holders into the Chinese market and gives Chinese firms bargaining power with foreign suppliers over technology and intellectual property. This strategy has been instrumental in the development of some new digital technologies to the advantage of Chinese (and Chinese Taipei) firms. Despite or because of the failure of some earlier attempts, Latin American governments dismantled their incipient industrial policies in the 1990s and only now are starting to reconsider them.

Nevertheless, the environment for innovation in China has several limitations, many of them similar to those found in most Latin American countries. Irksome procedures hinder starting new companies; access to credit and capital markets is very limited; property rights are weakly protected; and competition is restricted by geographical and infrastructure barriers that raise the cost of transport and by a multiplicity of local protection mechanisms for industries in the form of operating permits, requirements for use of local raw materials, taxes and other restrictions (World Bank, 2003*a*). This suggests that it is time to look at the other side of the mountain.

China's Weaknesses

The lack of separation between the state and the market is the overriding weakness of the Chinese economy. The state does not just simply interfere strongly in the decisions of other economic agents, as in Latin America before the wave of structural reforms of the last 20 years, but it is also the most important agent in domestic and international production as well as in marketing decisions. In fact, the state remains the main employer and the main channel for the allocation of savings. The lack of separation between the state and the market extends to all aspects of economic activity and is aggravated because the state is not a cohesive, centralised entity but a thousand-headed hydra that operates at all levels. It becomes evident in poor corporate governance, major risks in the financial sector and the use of a variety of controls that favour state-owned enterprises and reduce market discipline. Overinvestment in many sectors is a current manifestation of inadequate market discipline.

State-Owned Enterprises and Corporate Governance

In China it is not possible to define precisely the dividing line between public and private property. The introduction of non-state forms of production began with the system of rural responsibility that led to the privatisation of agriculture (although not rural land, which remains under state or community control) and to the proliferation of "town and village enterprises", small and medium-sized light manufacturing firms. The success of this experiment led the government in 1984 to initiate reforms in state industrial companies, which are continuing. The objective of the process was to improve efficiency in the state sector while preserving the state ownership of these companies. In the process, the Chinese state has experimented with an enormous variety of forms of state, collective, foreign and individual ownership, all of which currently coexist around a nucleus of large state companies, which in 2001 accounted for 47.3 per cent of investment in the fixed assets of the economy and 44 per cent of industrial production. Even by then, however, the number of state companies had fallen by two-thirds, to 34 500 from 87 900 in 1995, as a result of the "grab the big and let the small go" strategy announced by Zhu Rongji in 1998 (*China Economic Quarterly*, 2003, pp. 20). As a result, the share in value added of state-and collectively controlled firms in the business sector declined from 46.5 per cent in 1998 to 36.7 per cent in 2003 (OECD, 2005).

The last step in this reform process was the establishment in 2003 of the State-owned Assets Supervision and Administration Commission (SASAC), which currently exercises direct control over 169 large state companies, guaranteeing that the three largest firms in the main economic sectors remain state-owned and that 30 to 50 per cent of them will be "national champions" or "globally competitive" multinationals by 2010. This does not mean that the other state companies will necessarily be privatised, but rather that they will have to support themselves. An explicit reform objective is to expand state control capacity through the laws and regulations on ownership and corporate governance. The preferred way to restructure state companies throughout China is to set up an operating company to hold the productive assets. This company is in turn owned by a state-owned holding company. These holding companies exercise control and assume responsibility for the social obligations that all state companies had in the past (education, housing, social security). Many state-controlled operating companies offer shares on the stock market, a mechanism that in practice also contributes to expanding state control because the minority shareholders lack the rights common in other countries. In addition, the reliability of accounting systems and external auditing is very poor, and the practice of selling shares among holders to manipulate their value is rampant, according to the international indicators of the World Economic Forum. Moreover, the Corporation Law has been designed to facilitate the corporatisation of state companies, impose earnings reinvestment requirements and restrict the composition of boards of directors in ways detrimental to independent control of private companies[20].

Because state-owned enterprises are structured to respond more to the political and strategic objectives of the Communist Party than to market signals, it is not surprising that investment decisions, often flawed, lead to overinvestment. Foreign firms are also encouraged, especially by local governments through a variety of incentives, to invest in sectors that may bring political recognition. Excess capacity is rampant in steel, aluminium and cement, sectors under the control of the government, but it is also noticeable in automobiles, electronics, communications equipment and many other sectors with high foreign participation. The major risk caused by overinvestment is that many state-owned firms may find it impossible to honour their financial commitments to the already overextended official banks.

The Financial System

The financial system, without doubt the Achilles' heel of the Chinese economy, has traditionally served state companies. Although China has one of the deepest financial systems in the world — in 2004 the stock of domestic credit rose to 160.7 per cent of GDP and the value of the broader money supply in circulation expanded 184.9 per cent of GDP (EIU, 2006) — in practice access to credit is restricted to state-controlled companies and the largest private-sector firms. Small and medium-sized businesses, which account for more than half of GDP, receive less than 10 per cent of total bank loans (OECD, 2005)[21]. In the opinion of businesses consulted by the World Economic Forum, China restricts access to credit more than do most Latin American countries, where typical ratios are 30 per cent of GDP. Because equity-market access also tilts in favour of incumbent (especially state-owned) firms, efficient methods to allocate savings are clearly wanting.

The banking system is dominated by four major state banks originally oriented to separate sectors: the Bank of China, the China Construction Bank, the Industrial and Commercial Bank of China and the Agricultural Bank of China. The People's Bank of China operates as the central bank (and until recently as regulator of the banking system), and there are many state-owned commercial banks, most of them regional. Until 2003, only one private bank other than branches of foreign banks could offer international services. Since 2003, foreign banks have been able to provide services in local currency to Chinese companies, and at the end of 2006 they were authorised to offer services to individuals. Pursuant to commitments made by China on its accession to the World Trade Organization, the geographical restrictions on the operation of foreign banks were finally eliminated in 2006.

These limitations contrast with the freedom of entry and operation that has existed in most Latin American financial systems since the reforms of the 1990s. The main weakness of the Chinese financial system does not relate to these restrictions, however, but to the poor quality of regulation and supervision. According to official figures for the end of 2002, the non-performing debts of the four major state banks equalled 26 per cent of their assets. By September 2005, the non-performing loan ratio of the big four banks had declined to 10.1 per cent (EIU, 2005), due to policies adopted to clean their portfolios. The real bad-debt ratio is thought to be higher, however, because of the practice of refinancing financially troubled state companies at interest rates controlled by the government[22].

The government has taken several measures to deal with the problems of the major banks. In 1998 it gave them a $33 billion capital injection and transferred their bad debts to asset-management corporations for liquidation. In 2003, the Chinese Banking Regulation Commission was established and, in January 2004, a new capital injection of $45 billion went to two of the four largest state banks (Bank of China and China Construction Bank), which raised their capital to risk-weighted assets ratios from 7 per cent to 16 per cent (the international standard is 8 per cent). In 2005, a further $15 billion was injected into the Industrial and Commercial Bank of China and, in late 2005, the China Construction Bank became listed in Hong Kong, China and raised $8 billion from international investors. In 2006, the Bank of China and the Industry and Commerce Bank of China went public. ICBC public offering has become the largest in world history (around $22 billion) and its market capitalisation could be around $130 billion[23]. However, banks will likely remain under central government control and their management will stay exposed to political influences[24].

Many Latin American countries have experienced banking crises in the last 20 years, which have forced them to strengthen their systems of supervision and prudential regulation, raising them above levels current in China. Needless to say, the macroeconomic volatility characteristic of Latin American countries is a source of vulnerability that China has not had to face, at least so far. Yet ample evidence shows that financial liberalisations often turn sour in countries that lack adequate institutional infrastructure, because previous systems of interest-rate controls and directed credit may have created weak bank portfolios and failed to promote good "credit cultures" (Caprio and Hanson, 2001). Such concerns fully apply to China. Research on financial crises has also shown that when basic institutions that govern credit markets are flawed (i.e. when the rule of law is weak, creditors are unprotected and regulation is deficient) liberalisation increases the likelihood of a crisis (Demirgüc-Kunt and Detragiache, 1998; Arteta *et al.*, 2001). Thus, even as current conditions in the financial sector pose a threat to Chinese stability, reform and eventual liberalisation will not be risk-free either.

Given the difficulties of reforming the financial sector, equity-market liberalisation could in principle make a major difference in China. More financially developed countries experience larger than average boosts from equity-market liberalisation, which suggests that China could obtain an important benefit. Again, however, this effect tends to be muted in countries like China with poor legal systems and weak investor protection (Bekaert *et al.*, 2004).

The Trade Regime and International Transactions

Like Latin America, China has drastically cut tariffs and eliminated most restrictions on imports in the last 20 years. The average tariff rate fell from 43.3 per cent in 1985 to 12.7 per cent in 2002, a drop slightly slower than in Latin America but similar in scope (Yang, 2003). Shortly after Latin America did so, China unified its exchange market in 1994, and in 1996 it eliminated the main restrictions on foreign-exchange trading associated with international trade. In other respects, however, international goods and capital transactions remain subject to restrictions that do not exist in Latin America. Only authorised companies may engage in international trade transactions. Until 2005, regulations prevented privately owned firms from entering a number of sectors, such as infrastructure, public utilities and financial services. All incoming capital is deposited in a special account, and payments or transfers against these accounts require approval from the State Administration of Foreign Exchange (SAFE). Until early 2006, foreigners could invest only in B shares, which do not have the same rights as regular A shares. New rules allow some overseas investors to buy A shares as long as they purchase at least 10 per cent stakes in listed companies and hold the stock for at least three years. All outward capital operations require authorisation from SAFE, and Chinese investment abroad is regulated and controlled by the China Securities Regulatory Commission (OECD, 2003). However, also since 2006, some domestic investors (Qualified Domestic Institutional Investors, ODIIs) have been authorised to invest domestic funds in foreign markets. Therefore, China is starting to experiment, in a various cautious way, with a gradual liberalisation of its capital markets.

Misleading Indicators, Uncharted Paths

Given the lack of separation between the state and the market, one must interpret many economic indicators with caution.

For example, financial depth does not reflect ease of access to credit because the state largely controls the credit system. For the same reason, the total savings ratio is not a good indicator of the economy's investment capacity, or at least of investment capacity according to efficiency criteria. According to official statistics, China's saving and investment rates — at close to 50 per cent of GDP (or 44 per cent and 40 per cent of GDP, respectively, to accord with recent revisions to 2004 GDP[25]) — are among the world's highest and more than double the rates typical in Latin America. One might think that rapid economic growth is the natural result of such rates, but causality could go in the opposite direction. The real engine of growth functions through the movement of labour into the most efficient sectors, which have lower intensities of capital use than do the state companies and to a large extent finance their investments through external savings, i.e. from foreign investment.

Although the private sector has been the main source of growth, China is not evolving into a typical capitalist economy. The lack of separation between state and market encourages business leaders to create a corporatist association between companies and government. This will not lead to an expansion of space for private initiative on market conditions, but rather to a symbiosis of the interests of government and large private companies. A recent study found that over 40 per cent of private entrepreneurs in companies with annual incomes over one million renminbis ($120 800) have become members of the Communist Party, while only 5 per cent of the general population are party members. The growing numbers of business associations have also begun to play a similar role, supported by business people's conviction that they can influence official decisions (Dickson, 2003).

Common Weaknesses of China and Latin America

With its growing economic weight in the world, its high saving and investment ratios and its prodigious industrial capacity, China can seem like a developed country. Yet it remains an economy with low economic, social and institutional development and as such shares a series of weaknesses with Latin American countries. As economic development progresses, these weaknesses may become more troubling. Some observers even talk of an eventual "Latin Americanisation of China: the possibility that growing income inequalities and an ill-regulated rush to privatise could precipitate economic and political upheaval" (*The Economist*, 25 March 2006).

Limited and Unequal Education

The Chinese and Latin American labour forces currently have similar levels of education, a little less than six years on average, according to the well known Barro and Lee (2000) database. China has made rather more rapid progress than Latin America, but both regions have lagged behind the East Asian tigers and remain far below the average education level (ten years) of developed countries. As in Latin America, considerable regional inequalities mark education in China. For example, enrolment rates in junior secondary education vary from 49 per cent in Tibet and about 60-70 per cent in seven other lagging provinces to about 99 per cent in Beijing, Shanghai, Tianjin and Zhejiang. In the lagging provinces only 70 per cent of the students complete the nine-year compulsory education curriculum, compared with 100 per cent in East China (World Bank, 2003*a*)[26]. Many rural schools lack funds and must survive with fee donations from parents, a practice that the government hopes to eradicate by the end of 2007. Absenteeism and early school dropout are frequent despite the compulsory nine years of study.

As in Latin America, the improvement of education at low and middle levels is constrained on the supply side by limitations on resources and glaring organisational deficiencies and on the demand side by a lack of economic incentives to encourage families to keep their children in school. The emergence of economic opportunities, however, has raised the return on education, especially at the highest educational levels, again as in Latin America. For example, the gap between the returns on university and primary education rose from 25 per cent in the late 1980s to almost 80 per cent in the late 1990s (World Bank, 2003*a*). Income concentration has reflected these changes. The

Gini coefficient of income per capita increased from 0.35 in 1989 to 0.44 in 2000 (World Bank, 2003a), and to nearly 0.5 in 2005 according to some sources[27], not far from Latin America's average coefficient of 0.53 (De Ferranti *et al.*, 2003).

Another common feature of education structures in China and Latin America is the concentration of public expenditure at the tertiary level. In contrast with the United States or South Korea, where public spending per student is less at the tertiary than at the secondary level, Mexico and Chile spend more than twice as much on a university student than a secondary student. In China the gap is 5:1 (De Ferranti *et al.*, 2003). This reflects the priority that the government gives to higher education in a bid to speed up the country's technological progress. In 2004, China had 13.3 million university students, up from 5.6 million in 2000, engineering and management being the two most popular courses. China had 820 000 students in postgraduate programs (up from 301 000 in 2000), as well as 115 000 students studying abroad (EIU, 2006). Since nothing comparable is happening in Latin America, the education structures of the two regions seem likely to diverge.

Corruption and Weak Rule of Law

If anything is important for development, institutions and particularly respect for the law and control of corruption predominate (Easterly and Levine, 2002; Rodrik *et al.*, 2002; Dollar and Kraay, 2002). According to Kaufmann *et al.* (2005), respect for the rule of law in China falls well below the world average. It is on a level similar to those of El Salvador or the Dominican Republic and significantly below those of Chile, Costa Rica and Uruguay (Figure 1.3). This measure of the rule of law synthesises various indicators and expert opinions that reflect the degree of respect for rules, contracts, legal security and property, as well as the backing of the judicial system. On control of corruption China ranks even lower, on a level with the Dominican Republic, Jamaica and Honduras and substantially below Chile, Costa Rica and Uruguay (Figure 1.4). In this system of indicators, corruption means the unlawful appropriation of public resources for private purposes.

Although the rule of law is almost as weak in China as in the average Latin American country, the problem manifests itself with appreciable differences. In Latin America the homicide rate in the average country is 13 per 100 000 people; in China it is only 2.2 (IDB, 2000; Interpol, 2004). China also has low rates of other forms of violence and anti-social behaviour, such as robbery or sexual crime, which traditionally have been strongly punished. In

The Visible Hand of China in Latin America

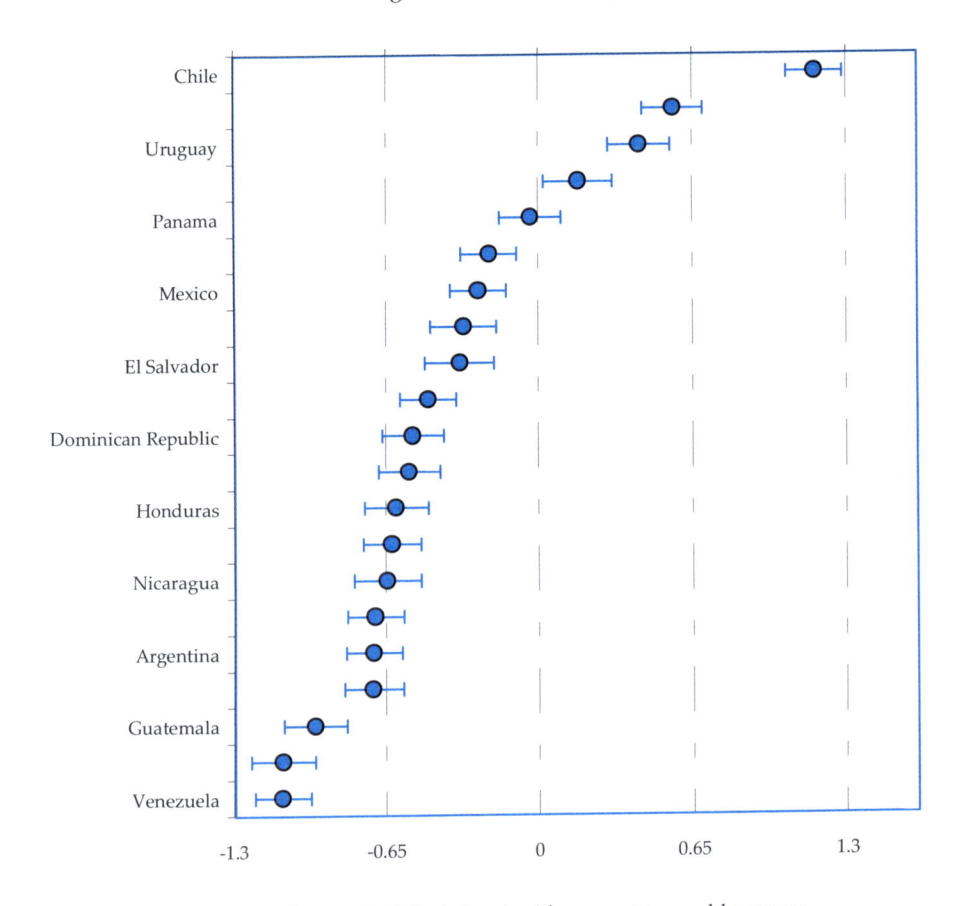

Figure 1.3. **Rule of Law, 2005**

Scale: Distance (in standard deviations) with respect to world average.

Dots represent central values and lines 95% confidence intervals for each country, based on a wide set of indicators.

Source: Kaufmann, Daniel, Aart Kraay and Massimo Mastruzzi (2003). "Governance Matters III: Governance Indicators for 1996-2002". World Bank Policy Research Department Working Paper.

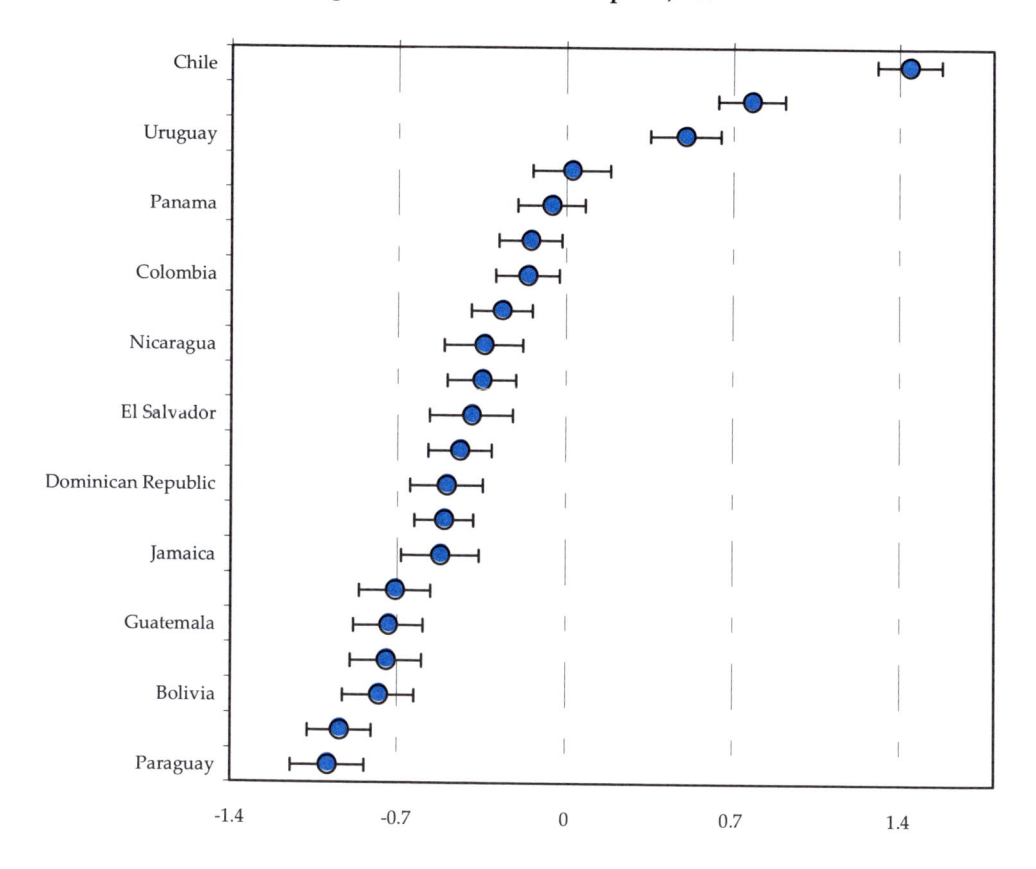

Figure 1.4. **Control of Corruption, 2005**

Chile	
Uruguay	
Panama	
Colombia	
Nicaragua	
El Salvador	
Dominican Republic	
Jamaica	
Guatemala	
Bolivia	
Paraguay	

Scale: Distance (in standard deviations) with respect to world average.

Dots represent central values and lines 95% confidence intervals for each country, based on a wide set of indicators.

Source: Kaufmann, Daniel, Aart Kraay and Massimo Mastruzzi (2003). "Governance Matters III: Governance Indicators for 1996-2002". World Bank Policy Research Department Working Paper.

China the weak rule of law becomes much more evident in the lack of secure property rights, especially in rural areas, the weakness of contracts and the unpredictability of judicial decisions.

Although the judicial systems of both China and Latin America suffer from serious weaknesses, these deficiencies have radically different origins. In Latin America, justice operates with complex and formalistic procedures derived from the Napoleonic Code that delay decisions, lessen their transparency and limit access to the courts. Because of this legalistic tradition, lawyers are numerous and play an important role in economic activities. China, on the other hand, has no tradition of this kind. During the Mao Zedong period the law remained subordinate to political ideology, and the judicial system hardly existed, although national and local authorities controlled summary judicial mechanisms and mediation systems.

Since 1978, a body of laws has been created by transplant from abroad with little adaptation, and an incipient legal tradition has slowly begun to emerge. In 1985, there were only 13 403 qualified lawyers in all of China, and half of them worked only part time. By 2000, the number had risen to 117 260, mainly full-time. Nonetheless, it is mistaken to think that the rule of law will prevail as a direct result of the number of lawyers, courts and cases settled. Except in some of the large coastal cities, most of the more than 200 000 judges in China are retired officials of the People's Liberation Army who lack legal training and independence. Even more serious, the incipient legal system seems alien to Chinese cultural tradition. As one report has noted, "In many respects it is like a transplant or graft that is in danger of being rejected by the many natural antibodies it encounters." (OECD, 2003, p. 113)

In both China and Latin America, legal gaps and the lack of consistency and credibility of judicial decisions militate against a broad-based system of innovation. Protection of intellectual property rights is weak and ineffectual. Even so, China has made substantial progress in the last 20 years by setting up specialised courts to deal with property rights, and a patent registration system has gained credibility, as reflected in the growth of applications (over 170 000 in 2000). Like Latin America, however, China has not yet assimilated a culture of respect for international intellectual property, while the rules for the protection of patents, trademarks and commercial rights are imprecise and of limited effect (OECD, 2003).

A judicial system such as China's is hardly immune to corruption. More generally, however, the problem of corruption in China stems from the omnipresence of the state in its attempt to control economic decisions to preserve the power of the Communist Party. The reform process initiated in the late 1970s has prompted continuous conflict between the need to create new spaces for decision making by economic agents to improve efficiency and the expansion of potential sources of illegal income in the effort to maintain state control over other spaces. The land-ownership control system still in force provides a good example. Corruption originates in two simple facts: all land is owned by the state, and administrative decision determines the value of rights of use. As a result, access to land is difficult without illegal payments to the district or municipal officials who control rights of use. A press source reported that 84 per cent of sales of land rights in Shanghai in recent years occurred through illegal mechanisms (*China Economic Quarterly*, 2003). Other recognised areas of corruption are residence permits, customs and banks. A striking and especially problematic feature of corruption in China lies in its growing decentralisation as a result of the erosion of central state control over sub-national entities and their officials in the wake of the growth and diversification of private economic activity[28].

Conclusion

China's rapid growth, its ability to attract foreign investment and its success as an exporter all cause concern among entrepreneurs and governments in Latin America. Although it is wrong to believe that good performance by one country comes at the expense of others, China is forcing Latin America rapidly to restructure some of its productive sectors in order to defend its position in international markets. This chapter has shown that China enjoys great strengths relative to Latin America, deriving from the size of its economy, the macroeconomic stability that it has enjoyed so far, the abundance of low-cost labour, the rapid expansion of its transport, electricity and communications infrastructure and its ability to innovate. Yet China also has weaknesses. Their principal source lies in the lack of separation between market and state, which explains the inefficiency of China's state enterprises, the deficiencies of its corporate norms and the fragility of its enormous financial system (the economy's high level of savings notwithstanding). In several ways the Chinese economy does not differ substantially from that of the typical Latin American country. The rule of law is weak and corruption is endemic. Education is poor and very poorly distributed, despite important scientific and technical advances at the university level. The lack of respect for property rights, the difficulty of starting businesses and the norms and practices that inhibit competition all conspire against innovation. Thus public institutions will be the battlefield in the attempt by both regions to attract foreign direct investment and create environments conducive to private initiative.

Notes

1. Eduardo Lora is Principal Research Advisor at the Inter-American Development Bank. This chapter is an abridged and updated version of a paper originally published in Spanish by *El Trimestre Económico*, Vol. LXXII (3), No. 287, July-September 2005, pp. 459-493.

2. The author acknowledges the editorial support provided by Juan Camilo Chaparro, Carlos Andrés Gómez-Peña and John Dunn Smith. Valuable comments by Andrea Goldstein, Roger Wilkinson and the members of the Inter-American Development Bank's (IDB) China Task Force are greatly appreciated.

3. Note that Young's calculations are for 1978-98, when annual growth was 9.1 per cent according to official figures. In the opposite direction, however, the results of a national economic census conducted in 2004 indicate that the economy is 16.8 per cent larger than previously reported and that growth rates between 1994 and 2004 were up to 1.5 percentage points higher than the official 9 per cent. See *Oxford Analytica*, "China: Census expands size of economy", 22 December 2005.

4. See Lall *et al.* (2004). Note, however, that according to Young manufacturing is the main source of overestimation of growth.

5. Competition for FDI between China and Latin America has been the subject of enquiry of some recent studies. A report by the Inter-American Development Bank (Devlin *et al.* 2006) assessed the evolution of cumulative bilateral FDI flows to Latin America and to China and calculated a coincidence index of the countries of origin of those flows. It concluded that competition appears to be low. A similar conclusion is reached by Chantasasawat *et al.* (2004). However, García-Herrero and Santabárbara (2007) [see Chapter 5 in this book] using econometric techniques, have found that the displacement effect is large and significant since 1995, and especially so for Mexico. Nonetheless, the issue is still open to further debate, as the effects found are implausibly large, probably as a result of the difficulty of adequately controlling for the numerous factors that may influence FDI flows.

6. *Oxford Analytica*, "Mexico: Maquiladoras Sector will Increase Activities", 29 March 2005.

7. FDI figures for Latin America come from CEPAL (2005) and for China from WDI (2005) and WEO (2006). However, caution must be exercised with FDI data for China, since income flows are affected by round tripping, that is the return as FDI of Chinese capital that has gone abroad to escape foreign exchange controls. It is estimated that between 30 and 50 per cent of FDI is round tripping. See Geng (2005).

8. For a comparison of factor endowments and export structures in China and Latin America, see Schott (2004). For a comparison of transportation costs and their role in export competitiveness, see Hummels (2004).

9. This ratio would fall to around 42 per cent with the recent revision of the size of the economy mentioned in note 3.

10. For the importance of market size in foreign direct investment, see IDB (2001), Chapter 18.

11. For a technical discussion of this result, see IDB (2001), Chapter 1.

12. Calculations based on data from *The Economist Intelligence Unit* and *The Economist* online.

13. Broad money supply (M2) grew by 18.7 per cent in 2003, 14.1 per cent in 2004 and 17.9 per cent year-on-year to September 2005. Source: The Economist Intelligence Unit (2005).

14. Calculation based on statistics from *China Statistical Yearbook 2005*.

15. National Bureau of Statistics of China, *China Statistical Yearbook*, various years.

16. For instance, while 67.7 per cent of local residents in a sample of five major cities have access to health insurance, just 12.4 per cent of migrants have it. See OECD (2005), p. 52.

17. According to World Bank (2003b) statistics, the median percentage of rural population in the region was 50.1 per cent in 1980 and 36.5 per cent in 2000.

18. According to these authors' calculations, Chile is the only country in which productivity contributed to growth in the 1980s and 1990s.

19. 1.2 per cent of GDP in 2004 according to the OECD.

http://www.oecd.org/document/26/0,2340,en_2649_201185_37770522_1_1_1_1,00.htm

20. However, the legal framework for the private sector will probably improve with a new bankruptcy law to be adopted in 2006 that is acknowledged to follow international best practice, and with the likely implementation of the 2004 constitutional amendment that recognised property rights.

21. According to Duenwald and Aziz (2003) loans to state companies in the strict sense were 67.6 per cent of GDP in 2000 out of a total equivalent to 124.6 per cent of GDP in that year.

22. According to "A Survey of China" published by *The Economist*, 25 March, p. 13, "UBS, an investment bank, reckons that the non-performing loan stock of the big four and other Chinese banks is now only around 30 per cent, half of its peak in the late 1990s (though that would still make China's one of the worst banking systems in Asia)".

23. The Economist Intelligence Unit (2005), p. 27. *The Economist* Online "A Dragon Stirs", 12 October 2006.

24. See *Oxford Analytica*, "China: Capital Injections Reflect Serious Intent," 12 January 2004, and "China: Party Stays in Charge Amid Bank Reform", 6 October 2005.

25. *Oxford Analytica*, "China: Census Expands Size of Economy", 22 December 2005.

26. The other lagging provinces are Guangxi, Guizhou, Hainan, Heilongjiang, Ningxia, Yunnan and Qinghai.

27. http://www.chinadaily.com.cn/english/doc/2005-06/19/content_452636.htm

28. Johnson (2004) provides a vivid recollection of cases of corruption with the tacit consent of the judiciary in local taxation and urban land rights.

Bibliography

Arteta, C., B. Eichengreen and C. Wyplosz (2001), "When Does Capital Account Liberalization Help More Than It Hurts?", *CEPR Discussion Paper* No. 2910, Centre for Economic Policy Research, London.

Barro, R.J. and J-W. Lee (2000), "International Data on Educational Attainment: Updates and Implications", mimeo, Harvard University, Cambridge, MA.

Bekaert, G., C.R. Harvey and C. Lundblad (2004), "Does Financial Liberalization Spur Growth?", *National Bank of Belgium Working Paper* No. 53, Brussels.

Brooks, R. and R. Tao (2003), "China's Labor Market Performance and Challenges", *IMF Working Paper* WP/03/210, Washington, D.C.

Caprio, G. and J.A. Hanson (2001) "The Case for Liberalization and Some Drawbacks", in G. Caprio, P. Honohan and J. Stiglitz (eds.), *Financial Liberalization: How Far, How Fast?*, Cambridge University Press, Cambridge, United Kingdom.

CEPAL (2005), *La Inversión Extranjera Directa En América Latina y El Caribe 2005*, CEPAL, Santiago de Chile, Chile.

CEPAL (various years), "Balance Preliminar de las Economías de América Latina y el Caribe", Santiago de Chile, Chile.

Chantasasawat, B., K.C. Fung, H. Iizaka and A. Siu (2004), *Foreign Direct Investment in East Asia and Latin America: Is there a People's Republic of China Effect?*, ADB Institute Discussion Paper No. 17.

China Economic Quarterly, 2003, 7(3).

De Ferranti, D., G. Perry, F. Ferreira and M. Walton, (2003), *Inequality in Latin America and the Caribbean: Breaking with History?*, World Bank, Washington, D.C.

Demirgüç-Kunt, A. and E. Detragiache (1998), "The Determinants of Banking Crises in Developing and Developed Countries", *IMF Staff Papers* 45(1): 81-109.

Devlin, R., A. Estevadeordal and A. Rodríguez (eds.), (2006), *The Emergence of China: Opportunities and Challenges for Latin America and the Caribbean*. Inter-American Development Bank, David Rockefeller Center for Latin American Studies, Harvard University.

DICKSON, B.J. (2003), *Red Capitalists in China: The Party, Private Entrepreneurs, and Prospects for Political Change*, Cambridge University Press, Cambridge, United Kingdom.

DOLLAR, D. AND A. KRAAY (2002), "Institutions, Trade and Growth", mimeo, World Bank, Washington, D.C.

DUENWALD, C. AND J. AZIZ (2003), "The Growth-Financial Development Nexus", in W. TSENG AND M. RODLAUER (eds.), *China: Competing in the Global Economy*, IMF, Washington, D.C.

EASTERLY, W. AND R. LEVINE (2002), "Tropics, Germs, and Crops: How Endowments Influence Economic Development", mimeo, Institute for International Economics, Washington, D.C.

ECONOMIST INTELLIGENCE UNIT (EIU) (2005), *China: Country Report*, Economist Intelligence Unit, London, December.

ECONOMIST INTELLIGENCE UNIT (EIU) (2006), *China: Country Profile 2006*, Economist Intelligence Unit, London.

The Economist (2006), 25 March and 30 March.

GARCÍA-HERRERO, A. AND D. SANTABÁRBARA (2007), "Does China Have an Impact on Foreign Direct Investment to Latin America?", Chapter 5 in this book.

GENG XIAO (2005), "Round-Tripping Foreign Direct Investment in the People's Republic of China: Scale, Causes and Implications", http://www.adbi.org/research-paper/2005/01/20/880.prc.fdi.rp/

HUMMELS, D. (2004), "The Role of Geography and Size", mimeo, Inter-American Development Bank, Integration and Regional Programs Department, Washington, D.C.

INTER-AMERICAN DEVELOPMENT BANK (IDB) (2000), *Development beyond Economics. Economic and Social Progress Report 2000*, IDB, Washington, D.C.

INTER-AMERICAN DEVELOPMENT BANK (IDB) (2001), *Competitiveness: The Business of Growth. Economic and Social Progress Report 2001*, IDB, Washington, D.C.

INTERNATIONAL MONETARY FUND (IMF) (various years), *World Economic Outolook Database*, IMF, Washington, D.C.

INTERPOL (2004), *International Crime Statistics*, http://www.interpol.int/Public/Statistics/ICS/downloadList.asp

JOHNSON, I. (2004), *Wild Grass: Three Stories of Change in Modern China*, Pantheon Books, New York, NY.

KAUFMANN, D., A. KRAAY AND M. MASTRUZZI (2005), "Governance Matters IV: Governance Indicators for 1996-2004", draft, World Bank, Washington, D.C., May.

KRUGMAN, P. (1994), "Competitiveness: A Dangerous Obsession", *Foreign Affairs* 73(2): 28-44.

Lall, D., M. Albaladejo and M. Mesquita (2004), "Latin American Industrial Competitiveness and the Challenge of Globalization", *IDB INTAL-ITD Occasional Paper* No. SITI-05, IDB, Washington, D.C.

Loayza, N., P. Fajnzylber and C. Calderón (2002), *Economic Growth in Latin America and the Caribbean: Stylized Facts, Explanations, and Forecasts*, World Bank, Washington, D.C.

Naughton, B. (2004), "China: Development Strategy and Policy Regime", mimeo, Inter-American Development Bank, Integration and Regional Programs Department, Washington, D.C.

Organisation for Economic Co-operation and Development (OECD) (2003), "China: Progress and Reform Challenges", *OECD Investment Policy Reviews*, OECD, Paris.

Organisation for Economic Co-operation and Development (OECD) (2005), "China", *OECD Economic Surveys*, Volume 2005/13, OECD, Paris, September.

Rodrik, D., A. Subramanian and F. Trebbi (2002), "Institutions Rule: The Primacy of Institutions over Geography and Integration in Economic Development", mimeo, Harvard University, Cambridge, MA.

Schott, P.K. (2004), "The Relative Revealed Competitiveness of China's Exports to the United States vis-à-vis other Countries in Asia, the Caribbean, Latin America, and the OECD", mimeo, Inter-American Development Bank, Integration and Regional Programs Department, Washington, D.C.

The Economist Intelligence Unit (2005), p. 27. The Economist Online "A Dragon Stirs", 12 October 2006.

United Nations (2002), *World Population Prospects: The 2002 Revision Population Database*, http://esa.un.org/unpp.

Wolf, M. (2003), "The Long March to Prosperity: Why China Can Maintain its Explosive Rate of Growth for Another Two Decades", *Financial Times*, 9 December.

World Bank (2003a), "China: Promoting Growth with Equity", Country Economic Memorandum, Report No. 24169-CHA, World Bank, Washington, D.C, 15 September.

World Bank (2003b), *World Development Indicators*, World Bank, Washington, D.C.

World BAnk (various years), *World Development Indicators Database*, World Bank, Washington, D.C.

World Economic Forum (WEF) (2006), *The Global Competitiveness Report 2006-2007*, WEF, Geneva.

Yang, Y. (2003), "China's Integration into the World Economy: Implications for Developing Countries", IMF Working Paper WP/03/245, IMF, Washington, D.C.

Young, A. (2003), "Gold into Base Metals: Productivity Growth in the People's Republic of China during the Reform Period", *Journal of Political Economy*, 111(6): 1220-1261.

Chapter 2

Angel or Devil? China's Trade Impact on Latin American Emerging Markets[1]

by Jorge Blázquez-Lidoy, Javier Rodríguez and Javier Santiso[2]

Abstract

China's economy has expanded by leaps and bounds, with dazzling progress since it first opened to foreign investment and reform in 1978. Over the last 25 years and after a long period of economic autarky the country has emerged as a major player in world trade. Its accession to the World Trade Organisation (WTO) in 2001 was a milestone. China presents both a threat and an opportunity for Latin American emerging markets. On average and despite some exceptions, Latin America is a clear trade winner from Chinese global integration. This chapter studies China's exporting and importing structure, using a database of 620 different goods. It builds two indices of trade competition to compare Chinese impacts over 1998-2004 on 34 economies, of which 15 are Latin American. The results generally confirm that there is no relevant trade competition between China and Latin America products in the US market. Not surprisingly, countries that export mainly commodities face lower competition, because China is a net importer of raw materials and an exporter of manufacturing products. At the same time, China is a wake-up call. The country has emerged as a major exporter at both the labour-intensive, low technology and, increasingly, at the knowledge-intensive, higher technology end of the product spectrum. It is presenting challenges to all developing countries, and particularly other trade champions like Mexico in nearly all sectors, from textiles to other more value-added industrialised products.

Introduction

Over the past two decades, China has become a major global economic player. Over the past twenty years its GDP has grown at the impressive rate of nearly 10 per cent a year according to official figures[3]. Its share of world merchandise trade has jumped from a meagre 1 per cent to more than 6.7 per cent in 2005. China's economic integration in the world economy has been impressive. In 2003, it was already the sixth-largest economy in the world at market exchange rates[4], the fourth-largest global trader and the major recipient of global foreign direct investment (FDI). If its trade growth holds, China will soon emerge as the third-largest trading economy in the world, overtaking Japan to rank behind just the United States and Germany.

As almost all Wall Street analysts underline, China's emergence has become the issue of the decade. It has had a direct or indirect impact on all raw material markets and therefore all developed or developing countries. China is on a charm offensive worldwide and especially in Africa where the China Development Bank, whose assets are bigger than the World Bank and Asian Development Bank combined, is extending its financial presence, along with commercial penetration by Chinese companies. Extravagant terms are *de rigueur* for discussing the country's 1.3 billion consumers. Goldman Sachs predicts that by 2040 China will overtake the United States as the world's biggest economy[5]. Much of the analysis may be overly optimistic. Some wonder if China's growth surge is driven by an investment bubble while others ring the "hard-landing" bell or worry about the Chinese currency peg[6] and the banking system[7]. For still others, China's developing capitalism is not solidly based on law, respect for property rights and free markets. Finally, it is unclear whether Chinese public banks allocate their capital according to capitalist economic criteria or whether they are vulnerable to negative shocks. The return to capital in China does not look very impressive either (Chong-En Bai, Chang-Tai Hsieh, Yingyi Qian, 2006). Quite evident, however, is the rush to the Chinese "gold mines" in all markets. Consider Chinese international bond issuances, for example. In mid-October 2004, China issued a €1 billion 10-year bond that was more than four times oversubscribed by large European investors ranging from Finnish pension funds to Italian asset managers. The spreads of 50-60 basis points over US Treasuries were largely comparable to those of investment-grade Chilean bonds and even to those of OECD developed countries, such as the 20 basis points paid by the Kingdom of Spain the same week or the 100 basis points paid by Poland (on China – and India – financial integration related issues, see Lane and Schmukler, 2006).

Economic historians would suggest, however, that China's boom and its emergence on the world economic scene are neither new nor without precedents[8]. China was the largest economy for much of recorded history, and until the 15th century it had the world's highest income per head. Even in 1820, when Europe had long before overtaken it in terms of GDP per person, it still accounted for 30 per cent of world GDP. Moreover, as the IMF underlines, one can easily compare recent Chinese experience to that of Japan or the Asian emerging economies; indeed, China's share of world trade remains far below Japan's, for example (IMF, 2004). The same study emphasises that China's rising share in world output and economic integration has had significant impacts all around the world – in Asia (see also Ahearne *et al.*, 2003) but also further afield in areas such as Latin America and Africa (on China's rising world impact see Hausmann Lim, and Spence, 2006).

The growing impact on Latin America has raised the interest of major institutions involved in both Asia and Latin America. Lall and Weiss (2004; and also in this volume) and Lin (2004) are both studies from the Asian Development Bank (ADB). Its Latin American counterpart, the Inter-American Development Bank (IDB), has multiplied its studies of the Chinese impact on Latin America (Lora, 2004*a*, for example, and also in this volume) and has developed a dense research network and an agenda to encourage Asia/Latin America research[9]. At the 2004 Annual IDB Meeting in Lima, the candidacy of China as a new member of the institution was made official, and the 2005 Annual IDB Meeting took place in Japan. On 1 October 2004, the IDB in co-operation with the ADB organised a major event on China and Latin America in Washington and published an extensive report (IDB, 2004). As the then President of the IDB, Enrique Iglesias, underlined, this was the first time in the history of the institution that such an event took place. The following years, ECLAC (the United Nations Economic Commission for Latin America and the Caribbean), the CAF (*Corporación Andina de Fomento*) (ECLAC, 2004; CAF, 2006), the IDB (IDB, 2006; and Devlin, Estevadeordal, and Rodríguez-Clare, 2006) and the World Bank (Lederman, Olarreaga and Perry, August 2006) released their analyses along with other US based think tanks and scholars (Domínguez, 2006) of China's impact on Latin America. In November 2005 Chile reached a free trade agreement with China, the first ever between the Asian giant and a Latin American country. Chile exports 36 per cent of its products to Asia.

Banco Bilbao Vizcaya Argentaria (BBVA), a major European bank with a large Latin American franchise, has published several pioneering studies of which Chapter 2 is an updated and expanded version, assessing the impact of

China on the region. Among them were articles in two issues of the BBVA monthly review, *Latinwatch*. Its June, 2003 issue contained an article entitled "Mexico and China in World Trade" suggested that the emergence of China as a trade global player was negative for Mexico; another article, "China's Economic Potential and Opportunities for Argentina" (*Latinwatch*, April, 2004 expanded in Blázquez and Santiso, 2004) found results for Argentina to be quite the opposite. That the same review published two case studies with contradictory results is, at the least, surprising. Perceptions of the impact of the emergence of China on Latin America do seem rather contradictory. On the one hand, China's very low labour costs and therefore strong competitiveness present a risk for other economies; on the other, China's enormous domestic market presents an opportunity. Is China an angel or a devil for Latin America?

This chapter assesses the short-term and long-term trade impact of China on Latin America derived from the emergence of China as a global player. It follows similar methodologies to those used by Rumbaugh and Blancher (2004), which studied the risks and opportunities of China's emergence on a global scale, but unfortunately excluded Latin America. Most studies of China's trade impact on emerging markets tend to concentrate on Asia, where Chinese exports tend to crowd out those of other Asian countries, as stressed by Eichengreen *et al.* (2004). In fact, much of the increase in US imports from China has occurred at the expense not of countries like Mexico or Central America (protected by proximity) but of Asian economies like Japan or the emerging economies of the area. For example, nearly 60 per cent of US shoe imports in 1988 came from South Korea or Chinese Taipei, compared with a meagre 2 per cent from China. By 2003, China had gained a share of more than 70 per cent while US imports from South Korea and Taiwan had faded away.

China's emergence as a global trader is in many ways exceptional in its speed and depth. China is already a much more open economy than most emerging markets. In 2005, the sum of exports and imports of goods and services reached more than 70 per cent of GDP, as against 30 per cent or less in the United States, Japan or Brazil, according to WTO data. Chinese trade performance in these terms is comparable, however, to that of some Latin American countries like Chile or Mexico (60-65 per cent) and of some developed countries like Spain.

The Emergence of China as a Global Trade Player

China's progress since it first opened to foreign investment and reform in 1978 has been dazzling. Its average annual GDP growth reached 9.7 per cent during 1978-2006[10]. Over the last 20 years and after a long period of economic autarky, the country emerged as a major player in world trade. During those years, China significantly reduced its tariffs and progressively joined the global trading system. Its 2002 weighted-average tariff was 6.4 per cent as against 40.6 per cent ten years before (Table 2.1). Its accession to the World Trade Organisation (WTO) in December 2001 was a milestone.

Table 2.1. **Chinese Tariffs**
(Per cent *ad valorem*)

Year	Unweighted Average	Weighted Average	Dispersion (standard deviation)	Maximum
1982	55.6			
1992	42.9	40.6		220.0
1997	17.6	16.0	13.0	121.6
2002	12.3	6.4	9.1	71.0

Source: IMF, *World Economic Outlook 2004*.

With commercial opening, China's shares of global markets, especially the developed-country markets, grew quickly (Table 2.2). By definition, this occurred at the expense of other economies. Compared to some Latin American countries, however, China's export growth looks less impressive. During the 1990s, for example, countries like Mexico, Chile and Costa Rica registered export growth rates more impressive than China's (Lora, 2004*b*; and Lora's Chapter 1 in this book).

Table 2.2. **Chinese Export Shares in Major Developed-Country Markets**
(Per cent)

	1960	1970	1980	1990	2000	2002
Japan	0.5	1.4	3.1	5.1	14.5	18.3
United States			0.5	3.2	8.6	11.1
EU	0.8	0.6	0.7	2.0	6.2	7.5

Source: IMF, *World Economic Outlook 2004*.

China's gain in market shares is one reason why most emerging countries perceive it as a tough trade competitor[11]. Some even blame China for the poor performance of their exports in recent years[12]. In fact, China is taking the place of other emerging countries in world markets (on this emergence and its impact see Bussière and Schnatz, 2006 for a good survey). This negative perception increased after 2001, when China finally joined the WTO. The accession opened global markets to Chinese goods, and the Chinese ability to compete successfully in those markets became even more obvious.

China's share of world merchandise exports has indeed increased rapidly over the last 20 years. It rose to 5 per cent in 2002 from 0.9 per cent in 1980, then climbed to 6.7 per cent in 2005. By the end of 2004 China had become the world's third biggest exporter after the United States and Germany. From 1990 to 2002, world exports grew by around 90 per cent and Chinese exports by around 425 per cent. China can produce goods of low added value at very low costs because it has a more abundant labour force than do other economies. For example, Chinese wages are one-fourth as high as those in Latin American countries on average. In 2005 the average Chinese monthly salary in manufacturing was $112, as against around $440 in Mexico and $300 in other urban *maquiladoras* districts of Central America like Costa Rica, El Salvador or Panama. The picture is also rapidly changing: according to the investment bank CLSA (a subsidiary of Calyon), average wages for a factor worker in China, combined with social security costs, differ within the country. In areas like Shanghai the combined figure at the end of 2006 was already $350 a month in 2005 and almost $250 a month in Shenzhen.

Yet all these facts might be interpreted too naïvely in an exclusively negative way. On the positive side, there are benefits to be had from trade with China. China has an enormous and expanding domestic market. The emergence of China entails long-term benefits from trade. Developing countries like those of East Asia, which have established strong trade and investment relations with China, could gain from this process.

China's Trade Structure

In order to analyse the short-term impact of China's evolving trade, it is first necessary to study the country's export and import structures. At the outset, however, one should note the gap between commodity exports and imports, which amounts to $30.4 billion. As the previous section implies, this trade imbalance is temporary. One can expect a more sustainable trade balance in the long term.

The analysis here used the UNCTAD database[13], which considers 620 different goods in the three-digit *Standard International Trade Classification*. We used the UNCTAD one-digit classification. On the export side (Table 2.3), three key sectors predominated in 2004: manufactured goods, machinery and transport equipment and miscellaneous manufactured goods. Together, they accounted for 87.4 per cent of total exports. Note the impressive evolution of machinery and transport equipment. In 1998 such merchandise amounted to 28 per cent of total exports. Six years later, it represented 46.6 per cent, i.e. an 18.6 per cent-point increase. In contrast, exports of miscellaneous manufactured goods are quickly losing their share.

Table 2.3. **Exports**

Exports	1998	1999	2000	2001	2002	2003	2004
Machinery & transport equipment	28.0	31.1	34.2	36.8	40.3	44.0	46.6
Miscellaneous manufactured goods	37.3	36.2	33.7	31.9	30.2	28.1	25.6
Manufactured goods	16.0	15.3	15.4	14.8	14.5	14.0	15.2
Chemicals products	5.4	5.1	4.6	4.7	4.5	4.2	4.2
Food & animals	5.8	5.4	4.9	4.8	4.5	4.0	3.2
Mineral fuel & lubricants	2.8	2.3	3.1	3.1	2.6	2.5	2.4
Commodities	2.1	2.1	1.9	1.9	1.8	1.6	1.6
Crude material (ex. Food&fuel)	1.7	1.8	1.6	1.4	1.2	1.0	0.9
Beverages & tobacco	0.5	0.4	0.3	0.3	0.3	0.2	0.2
Animal & vegetable oil/fat/wax	0.4	0.3	0.3	0.3	0.2	0.2	0.1

Source: Based on Intracen 2006.

For imports (Table 2.4), manufactured goods, machinery and transport equipment and chemical products are the relevant sectors. They accounted for 69.2 per cent of total imports in 2004. The relatively similar structures of exports and imports suggest that significant intra-industry trade takes place. This reflects how China has turned into a regional production centre and manufacturing point for re-exports. As with exports, imports of machinery and transport equipment are increasing rapidly, but manufactured goods are losing weight in the import structure. These data of course reveal no information on Chinese advantages or disadvantages. To study the impact on other countries, more detailed analysis is needed.

Table 2.4. **Imports**

	1998	1999	2000	2001	2002	2003	2004
Machinery & transport	38.8	40.5	40.3	42.3	45.3	45.9	44.4
Manufactured goods	22.5	21.2	19.0	17.7	17.2	16.2	13.6
Chemicals products	13.8	13.8	12.7	12.4	12.3	11.1	11.2
Miscellaneous manufactured	7.8	7.3	6.1	7.7	7.6	8.6	9.4
Crude material (ex. Food&fuel)	7.5	7.6	8.8	9.0	7.6	8.2	9.8
Mineral fuel & lubricants	4.9	5.5	9.2	7.2	6.6	7.1	8.6
Food & animals	2.7	2.2	2.1	2.0	1.8	1.4	1.6
Commodities	1.1	1.5	1.4	1.3	1.2	1.0	0.9
Animal & vegetable oil/fat/wax	0.6	0.4	0.2	0.1	0.2	0.3	0.4
Beverages & tobacco	0.1	0.1	0.2	0.2	0.1	0.1	0.1

Source: Based on Intracen 2006.

The Short-term Costs of Chinese Trade Competition

Although one may think that China will benefit other emerging economies in the long term, some costs could arise in the short-term. China competes with those economies in developing markets. For the Latin American countries, anecdotal evidence suggests that Mexico is a paradigmatic example of these short-term costs[14]. In order to assess them the authors have constructed two indices of trade competition. Their purpose is to compare the export structure of China with those of other emerging economies in a particular period. If the structures of two countries are quite similar, then trade competition is more likely. These indexes were built using the UNCTAD database and are modified versions of the well-known coefficient of specialisation (CS) and coefficient of conformity (CC):

$$CS = 1 - \frac{1}{2}\sum_n \left| a_{it}^n - a_{jt}^n \right|$$

$$CCm = \frac{\sum_n a_{it}^n a_{jt}^n}{\sqrt{\sum_n (a_{it}^n)^2 \sum_n (a_{jt}^n)^2}}$$

where a_{it} and a_{jt} represent the shares of goods "n" in total exports of country "i" and country "j" in period "t". One country will always be China and the other a selected economy. If two countries (i, j) have exactly the same exporting structures, then both indexes are equal to one.

In this case, the potential trade competition is high. Both indexes equal zero if there is no coincidence. The two indices, rather than one, ensure that the results are consistent[15]. CS and CC have been calculated to examine Chinese competition with 34 economies, of which 15 are Latin American, for each of the seven years from 1998 through 2004. To present the results simply, the two indices are combined; the result, labelled CI, is the arithmetic average of both indices (see Table 2.5 and Figures 2.1 and 2.2 below).

Table 2.5

	CS*	CC*	CI*	CI 2002**
Paraguay	0.08	0.02	0.05	0.07
Venezuela	0.10	0.03	0.06	0.10
Bolivia	0.12	0.04	0.08	0.11
Panama	0.11	0.06	0.08	0.11
Chile	0.14	0.04	0.09	0.11
Honduras	0.14	0.05	0.09	0.13
Russia	0.15	0.06	0.10	0.12
Uruguay	0.18	0.07	0.12	0.17
Peru	0.19	0.08	0.13	0.17
Argentina	0.20	0.08	0.14	0.17
Guatemala	0.24	0.11	0.17	0.16
Colombia	0.25	0.12	0.18	0.20
El Salvador	0.31	0.21	0.26	0.25
Brazil	0.30	0.21	0.26	0.28
Pakistan	0.30	0.26	0.28	0.32
Slovakia	0.40	0.23	0.31	0.33
Spain	0.42	0.22	0.32	0.34
Costa Rica	0.34	0.32	0.33	0.29
India	0.42	0.25	0.34	0.38
Japan	0.41	0.35	0.38	0.38
Philippines	0.40	0.37	0.39	0.33
Bulgaria	0.43	0.36	0.39	0.41
Croatia	0.45	0.34	0.40	0.42
Poland	0.44	0.35	0.40	0.46
Turkey	0.43	0.38	0.41	0.49
Indonesia	0.46	0.39	0.43	0.42
US	0.43	0.44	0.44	0.44
Romania	0.45	0.45	0.45	0.52
Singapore	0.45	0.52	0.48	0.43
Czech R.	0.50	0.52	0.51	0.43
Malaysia	0.48	0.57	0.53	0.46
Mexico	0.52	0.54	0.53	0.50
Korea	0.50	0.60	0.55	0.48
Hungary	0.54	0.66	0.60	0.55
Thailand	0.57	0.71	0.64	0.57

*Average 2002-2004
**Average 2000-2002

Source: own data, 2006.

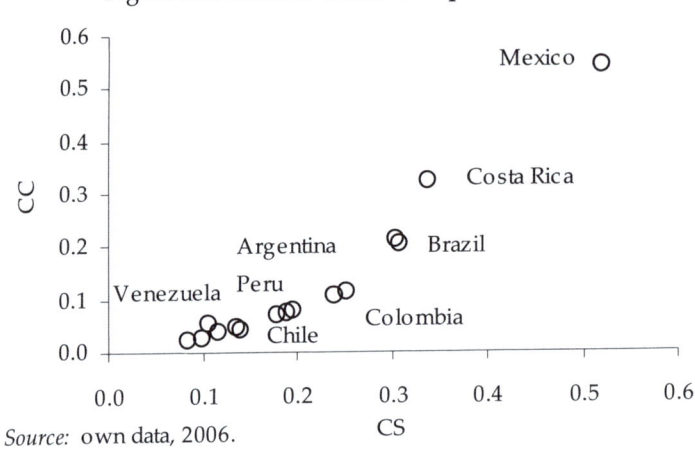

Figure 2.1. **Chinese Trade Competition**

[Scatter plot with CS on x-axis (0.0 to 0.6) and CC on y-axis (0.0 to 0.6). Countries shown: Mexico, Costa Rica, Brazil, Argentina, Peru, Venezuela, Colombia, Chile.]

Source: own data, 2006.

Figure 2.2. **Chinese Trade Competition**

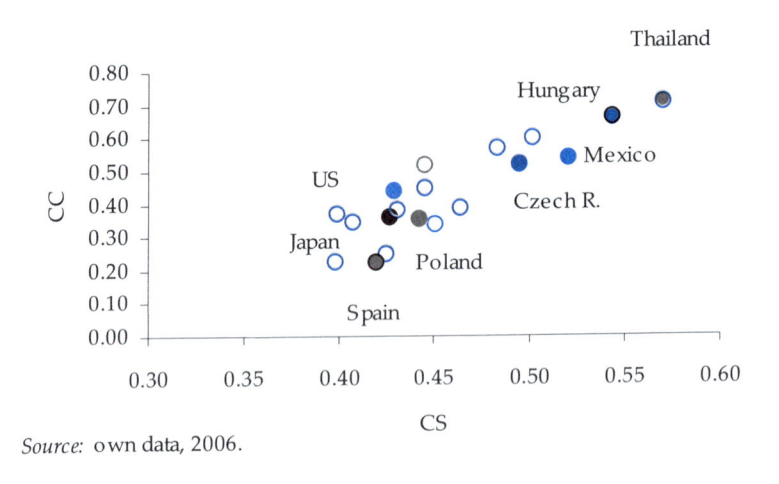

[Scatter plot with CS on x-axis (0.30 to 0.60) and CC on y-axis (0.00 to 0.80). Countries shown: Thailand, Hungary, Mexico, Czech R., US, Japan, Poland, Spain.]

Source: own data, 2006.

The results show relatively low figures for all Latin American economies except Mexico and Central America. In general, they suggest no trade competition between China and Latin America. Not surprisingly, countries that export mainly commodities face lower competition, because China is a net importer of raw materials. Paraguay, Venezuela, Bolivia and Panama exhibit the lowest figures among the 34 economies, i.e. they suffer least from Chinese trade competition. Brazil appears as an intermediate case between Mexico and Venezuela.

In a comparison of Latin American and other emerging countries, particularly in Asia, Chinese competition is not a problem in general terms with the possible exception of Mexico. Because of its comparative advantage in raw materials, Latin America is seemingly one of the most complementary regions for the Asian dragon. The value of Venezuelan crude shipments to China, for example, exceeded $3 billion in 2005, or twice the year before. While the United States is still the largest importer of Venezuelan crude, growing Sino-Latin American relations, in particular between Beijing and Caracas, have not gone unnoticed. In 2006, Venezuela and China signed an agreement related to oil exports from the former to the latter. Galloping demand from China assures that these increasing linkages are likely to continue unabated. China is the second largest importer of oil in the world, having overcome Japan in 2003. With ever-more Chinese buying cars, the OECD International Energy Agency predicts that China will need to import 80 per cent of its oil by 2030. The same applies to other commodities as different as copper or soybean, all of them among the many primary products exported by Latin American countries. In the three years to 2005, China accounted for 50 per cent of the increase in world consumption of copper and aluminium, and almost all the growth in nickel and tin.

Thus, one may conclude that Latin America faces few if any short-term trade costs. In fact, most Latin American countries are enjoying a tremendous increase in their exports to China. China has become Brazil's fastest-growing export market, for example, purchasing 80 per cent more from Brazil in 2003 than in 2002. Their bilateral trade has more than quadrupled over the past four years. Five commodities – soybeans, iron ore, steel, soy oil and wood – accounted for 75 per cent of Brazil's exports to China last year. China bought 6.2 per cent of Brazil's $73 billion of exports in 2003, up sharply from 1.4 per cent in 1999. Aracruz, Latin America's largest wood-pulp maker, has more than doubled its sales to China in the past two years to reach 12 per cent of the company's exports[16]. Another issue for Brazil is one of economic dynamics. China will continue to expand its exports, gaining market share in third markets for new products. From this perspective, as underlined by Brazilian economists (e.g. Paiva de Abreu, 2005), some Brazilian sectors like iron and steel products might face Chinese competition in the medium term. In a longer-term view, the automobile industry may do so as well.

Mexico clearly presents another story. The results (see Figure 2.3) show that Mexico faces strong commercial competition from China[17]. In fact, only Korea, Hungary and Thailand suffer from tougher competition. Anecdotal evidence supports this formal analysis. Moreover, Chinese trade competition is increasing over time, as the synthetic index (CI) shows[18]. China could indeed jeopardise some Mexican exports in foreign markets. The United States is by far Mexico's largest export market. It absorbed more than 85 per cent of Mexican exports in 2005[19]. In 2003, US trade data showed China's market share at 12.1 per cent, beating Mexico for the first time in its history. The Mexican share of the US market decreased to 11 per cent in 2003 from 11.6 per cent in 2002. Berges (2004) also documents these trends in detail, while other recent studies, using gravity-model analysis, confirmed the trade impacts of Chinese booming exports on Mexico. Had China's exports capabilities remained unchanged, they conclude, Mexico's annual export growth rate would have been 3 percentage points higher in the early 2000s (Hanson and Roberston, 2006).

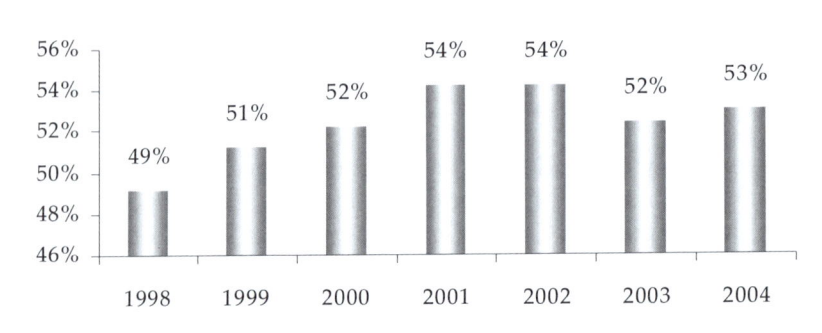

Figure 2.3. **Chinese Commercial Competition with Mexico**

Year	Value
1998	49%
1999	51%
2000	52%
2001	54%
2002	54%
2003	52%
2004	53%

Source: own data, 2006.

Mexico specialises in information technology (IT) and consumer electronics, electronic components, clothing, transport equipment and miscellaneous manufacturing, according to the Balassa index[20], which measures revealed comparative advantage. It compares the share of a given sector in national exports with its share in world exports. If the index is above one then a country is specialised in that sector. Table 2.6 shows the index values for both Mexico and China in 2002 and 2004 for 14 different sectors. China specialises in IT and consumer electronics, electronic components, clothing, miscellaneous manufacturing, textiles, basic manufactures and leather products. China and Mexico therefore specialise in similar sectors. From the Mexican point of view, transport equipment is the only one in which Chinese competition is not relevant.

Table 2.6. **Specialisation Index (Balassa)**

	China 2002	China 2004	Mexico 2002	Mexico 2004
Wood products	0.45	0.43	0.26	0.26
Leather products	3.70	3.34	0.34	-
Chemicals	0.46	0.42	0.35	0.34
Processed food	0.57	0.47	0.57	0.56
Textiles	2.43	2.39	0.53	0.49
Minerals	0.29	0.28	0.83	1.06
Basic manufactures	1.01	0.96	0.76	0.69
Non-electronic machinery	0.52	0.52	0.82	0.84
Fresh food	0.77	0.68	0.69	0.80
Miscellaneous manufacturing	*1.59*	*1.48*	*1.08*	*1.07*
Transport equipment	0.25	0.27	1.43	1.34
Clothing	*3.65*	*3.46*	*1.39*	*1.29*
Electronic components	*1.04*	*1.04*	*1.49*	*1.53*
IT & Conusmer electronics	*2.00*	*2.43*	*1.81*	*1.75*

Source: Own data based on Intracen 2006.

Some economists argue that the Mexican exporting model could be at risk. After the North American Free Trade Agreement (NAFTA) came into force in 1994, Mexico specialised in low added-value manufactures, i.e. *maquilas*. China can produce these kinds of goods at lower cost than Mexico.

Chinese competition will probably cause Mexico's current export structure to change. Singapore, Chinese Taipei and South Korea have already made such moves by reducing their exports of manufactured goods, machinery and transport equipment. Chemical and energy products (gas, oil and electricity) are gaining weight in their exports. Nevertheless, it is difficult to foresee the direction of change in Mexico's trade and to assess the future impact of China if one considers dimensions other than production and labour costs. Mexico clearly has one major competitive advantage over China, namely proximity to the US market. Many economists have stressed the importance of transport and trade costs in order to capture the penalty of distance (see Hummels, 2001*a*). Distance introduces delays in trade and raises freight and transaction costs. As Harrigan and Venables (2004) and Hummels (2001*b*) argue, an important element of distance costs in trade is time, i.e. the time needed to deliver intermediate and final goods. Time costs not only are quantitatively important, but also affect quality in terms of synchronising activities and delivery. Proximity thus creates incentives for clustering activities. Mexico probably should consider identifying sectors and products where distance and time are key comparative and competitive assets.

Evans and Harrigan (2003) developed a theoretical model in which timely delivery matters and products are therefore developed near the source of final demand, raising wages as a result. In their model timely delivery is a key asset, both because it allows retailers to respond quickly and efficiently to fluctuating final demand without holding costly inventories and because it is possible only where production located near final demand. This model is consistent with empirical examples and trends during the 1990s that witnessed some shifts in production locations away from lower-wage producers like China towards higher-wage locations like Mexico. This shift occurred, for example, in US apparel sourcing, and it is concentrated precisely on goods where timeliness of delivery is essential. Based on detailed empirical data from a major department store, the authors found strong evidence that nearby producers specialised in goods where time and timeliness matter as their model predicts.

One can argue that for Mexico reducing trade costs could restore a strategic NAFTA advantage because trade costs have become much more important than production costs (Deardoff, 2004). Some studies find a modest decrease in the elasticity of trade to distance, although most of them point to little or no change and more surprisingly to a modest increase (Disdier and Head, 2004). Gravity-equation estimates from panel data over long temporal horizons tend to find an increase (Brun *et al.*, 2005). Anderson and van Wincoop (2003) find trade costs on average nearly twice as large as production costs. This implies that trade costs are significant determinants of comparative advantage, perhaps even more than the production costs in which China has its competitive advantage.

In fact, and contrary to conventional wisdom, the effect of distance on trade has not only decreased but rather increased in recent decades (for a survey, see Anderson and van Wincoop, 2004). Hummels (1999) provided evidence using detailed data on shipping costs that ocean freight rates have increased while US air cargo rates indicate large cost reductions between 1955 and 1997 (a result confirmed for overland US transport costs by Glaeser and Kohlhase, 2003). Hence the reduction of transport costs does not seem uniform over time. Berthelon and Freund (2003) show that distance had a significant and increasing impact on trade in more than 25 per cent of 770 industries studied, with almost no industries for which distance became less important. Carrère and Schiff (2003) reached a similar conclusion from examining the level and evolution of countries' trade distances. They found that the distance of trade (DOT), an indicator of a country's proximity to the world centre of economic activity, decreased over time for a majority of countries with the exception of the United States during 1962-2000. In other words, countries still benefit from proximity to the centre of world activity while others are penalised for being far from it. In a systematic survey of empirical research on how distance effects have fallen or not over time (856 distance effects examined in 55 papers), Disdier and Head (2004) found that the negative impact of distance on trade has not shrunk but increased over the last century.

An issue for Mexico as well as other Latin American countries will be to reduce transport costs and boost infrastructure efficiency. For most Latin American countries, transport costs present even greater barriers to US markets than import tariffs[21]. In a detailed analysis of shipping costs to the US market, using a database of more than 300 000 observations per year on product shipments, Clark *et al.* (2004) found that port efficiency is an important determinant of shipping costs[22]. This becomes more relevant with the lowering of average tariff barriers. In both Asia and in Latin America, the relative importance of transport costs as a determinant of trade has increased. Excluding Mexico, average Latin American freight costs are similar to those of Asian competitors and in some cases even higher.

For countries like Chile or Ecuador transport costs exceed the average tariffs they face in the United States by more than 20 times. Lowering transport costs and thereby increasing infrastructure efficiency could boost Latin American trade performance[23]. Focusing on the effects of port efficiency on transport costs, Clark *et al.* (2004) found that improving port efficiency from the 25th to 75th percentiles would reduce shipping costs by more than 12 per cent. For Mexico, which benefits from US proximity, an improvement in port efficiency to the levels of countries like France or Sweden would reduce transport costs by around 10 per cent. Brazil or Ecuador would find their maritime transport costs reduced by more than 15 per cent. Latin America is perceived as having some of the least efficient ports. It also has significant customs problems, with a median clearing delay of seven days (the worst performers being Ecuador at 15 days and Venezuela at 11 days), high costs of handling containers inside the ports and important organised-crime activity in the seaport infrastructure. Clearly there is scope for improvements. The more than 12 per cent reduction in shipping costs cited above would equal 8 000 kilometres in distance reduction according Clark *et al.* (2004).

The Short-term Opportunities: China's Strong Demand

As we have seen, China's impact on Latin America is generally positive, with a few exceptions. Yet even for the exceptions – countries like Mexico that face increasing competitive pressure from China in the US market – China could, at least in theory, present opportunities as a potential export market for intra-industry trade exchanges. To assess such potential benefits from increasing Chinese demand, the analysis that follows uses two new indices based on the UNCTAD database described above. We compare the export structures of 15 Latin American countries with the import structure of China. If a particular country's exports are similar to Chinese imports (i.e. the index value approaches one), an obvious commercial opportunity and a potential trade gain would exist for the Latin American country, even if that country may not necessarily export to China currently. The indices are, again, modified versions of the well-known specialisation coefficient (CSm) and the conformity coefficient (CCm):

$$CSm = 1 - \frac{1}{2}\sum_n \left| a_{it}^n - a_{jt}^n \right|$$

$$CCm = \frac{\sum_n a_{it}^n a_{jt}^n}{\sqrt{\sum_n (a_{it}^n)^2 \sum_n (a_{jt}^n)^2}}$$

where a_{it} represents the share of goods "n" in total exports of the Latin American country "i" in period "t" and a_{jt} is the share of goods "n" in total Chinese imports in the same period. Both indices are equal to one if there is a perfect correspondence between Chinese imports and the exports of the Latin American country under consideration. Two indices again ensure consistency of the results, and the seven-year period is the same (1998-2004) with each year calculated separately. For presentation, a single aggregated index (Cim) is calculated in the same way.

Table 2.7 presents the results. Many Latin American countries are commodity exporters, and their potential trade with China concentrates in small baskets of goods. In other words, except for Mexico, intra-industry trade is not very likely with Latin America, given its export structure. Table 2.8 shows the Balassa export-specialisation indices for seven larger countries of the region:

Table 2.7. **Potential Trade with China, 2002-2004**

	CSm*	CCm*	Cim*	Cim 2002**
	0.09	0.03	0.06	0.08
Honduras	0.13	0.04	0.08	0.08
Paraguay	0.10	0.08	0.09	0.10
Peru	0.16	0.09	0.13	0.15
Bolivia	0.16	0.09	0.13	0.14
Uruguay	0.18	0.07	0.13	0.15
Chile	0.17	0.12	0.15	0.17
El Salvador	0.21	0.11	0.16	0.17
Guatemala	0.24	0.14	0.19	0.16
Venezuela	0.17	0.30	0.23	0.25
Costa Rica	0.24	0.25	0.25	0.25
Colombia	0.25	0.28	0.27	0.27
Argentina	0.31	0.23	0.27	0.30
Brazil	0.40	0.33	0.36	0.36
Mexico	0.44	0.50	0.47	0.47

*Average 2002-2004   **Average 2000-2002

Source: Own data, 2006.

Table 2.8. **Specialisation Index (Belassa)**

	(1)	(2)	(3)	(4)	(5)	(6)	(7)
Wood products	0.44	**2.13**	**4.53**	0.76	0.27	0.59	
Leather products	2.61	3.68		1.21	0.34		
Chemicals	0.75	0.63	0.63	**1.09**	0.35	0.35	0.48
Processed food	**5.57**	**3.11**	**2.68**	**1.50**	0.51	**5.24**	0.29
Textiles	0.34	0.60	0.25	0.88	0.52	0.80	
Minerals	**1.42**	0.69	**1.33**	**2.68**	0.67	**1.80**	**6.69**
Basic manufactures	0.79	1.44	3.68	0.92	0.74	3.18	1.30
Non-electronic machinery	0.30	0.75	0.08	0.11	0.75	0.14	
Fresh food	**5.58**	**3.84**	**4.01**	**4.24**	0.77	**2.49**	0.28
Miscellaneous manufacturing	0.30	0.34	0.20	0.49	1.10	0.33	0.06
Transport equipment	0.68	**1.13**	0.12	0.32	**1.43**		0.09
Clothing		0.15		1.47	1.52	2.73	
Electronic components	0.10	0.24	0.05	0.19	1.56	0.06	
IT & Consumer electronics		0.38			1.96		

Source: Own data based on Intracen 2006.

Argentina (1), Brazil (2), Chile (3), Colombia (4), Mexico (5), Peru (6) and Venezuela (7). The figures in bold type represent the sectors in which Latin America specialises and China does not, i.e. wood products, processed food, minerals and perishable goods – largely raw materials and their derivatives. Colombia also specialises in chemicals[24] and Mexico and Brazil in transport equipment. Table 2.9 indicates the shares of four broad commodity groups in Latin American exports.

Table 2.9. **Latin American Exports**
(% of total)

	Foods	Fuels	Metals	Manufactures
Mexico	6	10	2	81
Brazil	31	1	9	54
Argentina	49	12	2	34
Colombia	32	31	1	31
Peru	35	7	39	17
Chile	25	1	48	16
Venezuela	2	83	2	12

Source: Based on LatinFocus 2005.

Furthermore, trade with China could entail deeper specialisation for most Latin American exports because of China's current strong demand for commodities. In fact, China is becoming a global demander of raw materials. In 2003 it was already the world's largest importer of cotton, copper and soybeans and the fourth largest importer of oil[25]. Its demand for raw materials has been growing (Table 2.10). The combination of heavy industrial expansion and a booming economy has also created a huge, escalating demand for oil that suppliers strain to meet; China has leapfrogged Japan to become the world's second-largest oil consumer, just behind the United States.

Table 2.10. **Rate of Growth of Imports**
%, yearly average 1997-2002

	China	World
Soybean	75	11
Copper	63	5
Oil	19	2

Source: Based on USDA, *World Metal Statistics* and BP, 2005.

With trade concentrated in a small basket of commodities, China's strong demand for raw materials is thus good news for Latin America, a positive demand shock[26]. Moreover, even if direct trade with China does not rise, the favourable effect remains because of commodity price effects. If China increases its demand for crude oil, for example, oil-producing countries will raise their production, or prices will increase. By 2006, China's growing thirst for oil, combined with other international factors, was driving oil prices to their highest levels since oil futures started trading on the New York Mercantile Exchange in 1983. China alone accounted for nearly 40 percent of the entire growth in world oil demand from 2000 to 2003 (CERA, 2004)[27].

The four main Latin American commodities are copper, oil, soybeans and coffee. Together they account for 66 per cent of the region's total exports of raw materials. Excluding coffee, China absorbs an important share of these commodities. Latin America is also an important world producer of commodities. It produces 47 per cent of the world soybean crop, 40 per cent of global copper output and 9.3 per cent of crude oil output. Thus, to sum up, if vigorous Chinese demand continues to hold over time, a positive impact on the region is very likely, and one should expect deeper specialisation, with Latin America remaining exposed to terms-of-trade shocks.

The Chinese Impact on Trade in the Long Term

In the long term, as economic theory predicts, Chinese growth and the resultant increase in world trade will benefit other countries. The IMF's *World Economic Outlook* (2004) presents alternative scenarios of China's impact on world trade and growth. Although they should be interpreted cautiously, both show positive impacts on the rest of the world in the long term. Most regions will benefit from stronger demand generated by China's rapid growth, although places where labour faces stronger competition from China will benefit less. This study emphasises that countries benefiting the most will be those that are structurally more flexible. Ianchovichina and Martin (2003) present similar results.

China's emergence as a global trade player is not without precedent[28]. Consider the Japanese experience of the 1950s and 1960s[29]. After WWII the country was devastated and certainly characterised by its relatively low salaries. For more than 20 years Japanese economic policy boosted growth and turned Japan into the world's second largest economy. By the beginning of the 21st century, Japan was a key economy, representing around 9 per cent of world GDP (Figure 2.3). It is clear now that the performance of the Japanese economy benefited the world economy as a whole – Latin America included. In some ways, the evolution of the Chinese economy resembles the Japanese experience, with a clear correspondence between them. Both countries have had high-growth periods in which economic expansion averaged 8.5 per cent a year – 1952-1972 for Japan and 1979-1999 for China, with average annual growth of trade[30] at around 13 per cent[31]. Both countries gained weight in the world economy and contributed to it at similar rates. During 1952-1972, world GDP grew on average by 5.8 per cent, and Japanese GDP performance explained 0.6 points of that growth. During 1979-1999 China contributed 0.6 points of average annual world growth of 3.7 per cent.

Nevertheless, some outstanding differences appear in the Japan-China comparison. The composition of GDP was quite similar in the early 1950s in Japan and in the early 1980s in China (Table 2.11). Consumption accounted for around 60 per cent of GDP, investment for 15 per cent and net exports for over 25 per cent[32]. These shares changed with a significant divergence between the two countries. In Japan, the shares of consumption and net exports gave way to investment, but in China increases in both investment and net exports replaced a decreased consumption share. These figures reveal why China is perceived as a rival instead of a trade partner. China exports much more than it imports relative to GDP, so other countries perceive that Chinese growth is not spreading. This situation is not sustainable in the long-term. Eventually, China will import massively and net exports will fall[33]. According to the WTO database, China's merchandise imports in 2002 totalled 4.4 per cent of world imports, and its exports amounted to 5 per cent of world exports. The difference amounted to $30.4 billion, similar to the nominal GDP of Ecuador. By the 2005/06 Chinese manufacturers were already lapping up imports and dictating global prices of nearly everything from iron ore to microchips.

In another important difference between the two countries, Japan began with a more developed economy. China was and still is a developing one (Figure 2-4). Chinese GDP per capita in 2000 was around 50 per cent below the world average, similar to that of Ecuador according to the Summers and Heston database[34]. This suggests that despite its impressive performance over the last 20 years, deeper convergence might take some time. In other words, China could still enjoy a high rate of growth for a long period. The simple projections in Table 2.12 suggest the future weight of China in the world economy[35]. In the 1990s China grew by 10.1 per cent a year on average, the world by 3.3 per cent and Latin America by 3.4 per cent. If these rates hold for

Table 2.11. **Components of GDP**
(% of total GDP)

Japan	1953	1972
Consumption	60	53
Investment	14	35
Net Exports	26	11
China	**1979**	**1999**
Consumption	57	47
Investment	17	21
Net Exports	27	32

Source: Based on Summers and Heston database. See for a 2006 update of the database http://www.bris.ac.uk/Depts/Economics/Growth/summers.htm

the next 20 years, China will become the largest economy, beating by far the United States. One can also view the same kinds of simple projections from another perspective. Chinese imports of goods represent 4.4 per cent of world imports. During the 1990s, they climbed by around 16 per cent a year on average while world imports (ex-China) rose by about 7 per cent a year. If these figures hold, China will account for 8 per cent of world imports in 2010 and for 18 per cent of them in 2020.

Figure 2.4. **Share of World GDP**

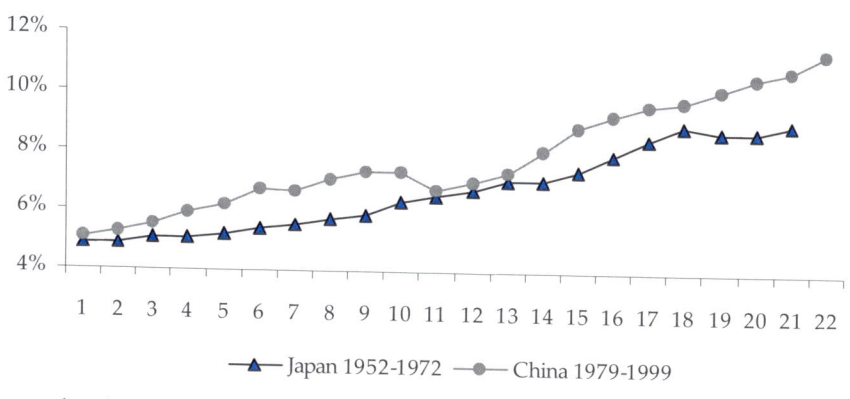

Source: based on Summer and Heston database.

Table 2.12. **Share of World GDP (%)**

	2002	2010	2020
China	12.7	21.1	40.1
Latin America	7.9	7.9	8.0

Source: Own data, 2006.

While it is hard to foresee in detail the long-term impact of China's emergence on other economies and on international trade, the aggregate impact has to be positive. It also could be asymmetric. Some sectors could benefit and others be harmed by Chinese competition. China has a competitive advantage in labour-intensive sectors, whose potential benefits are lower. The opposite applies to capital-intensive sectors (IMF, 2004).

Conclusions

The Chinese trade impact on Latin America is generally positive in the short and medium term. These results are consistent with others (e.g. IMF, 2004; Lall and Weiss, 2004 and this volume). On average, Latin American trade will benefit from increased Chinese demand and growth. In comparative terms, as the IMF (2004) notes, the only net loser could be South Asia, while Latin America is likely to feel a positive effect. For a sector like Latin American agriculture, the estimated impact of faster Chinese integration by around 2020 is clearly positive, with output up by 4 per cent. Clear losers, however, will be sectors like textiles and countries specialised in exports of labour-intensive manufactures. More detailed analysis would be needed to assess China's trade impact on the home markets of Latin American countries like Mexico. Clearly Latin American countries will have to upgrade their comparative advantage in proximity to the US, their major export market. For that they will need to boost the quality of their infrastructures. They will have also to concentrate on industries where this distance-time factor is an asset and try to move towards more value added products. At the same time, and for some of them, they will have to deal with the risks to be stuck in a raw materials corner that is also a poor provider of employment. Beyond China, the challenge will also come from India, a country that has been deepening its trade and financial ties with Latin America and its getting more integrated into the world. Using similar methodologies and approaches as those used in this chapter, Saaed Qreshi and Wan have analysed this growing impact (Saaed Qreshi and Wan, 2006).

In order to complete the picture, more studies will also be needed, and in particular studies looking at the growing intra-industry trade in intermediate goods and the opportunity that Asian drivers like China – and India – could represent for Latin American countries (for a specific case study focused on Argentina, see Castro, Tramutola, and Monat, 2005). Recent studies are also exploring how exploring the extent to which the rapid growth of China and India are affecting Latin America's trade specialisation (Lederman, Olarreaga, and Rubiano, 2006). Their results suggest that the specialisation pattern of Latin American economies, with the exception of Mexico, has been moving in the opposite direction to the trade pattern specialisation of China and India. Labour-intensive sectors, both skilled and unskilled, have been more negatively affected by the emergence of China and India, whereas natural resource and scientific knowledge-intensive sectors have been benefiting from their surge.

For countries like Brazil, for example, that have been able to develop a strong manufacturing and industrial base, a remaining challenge is to maintain the same type of exports to China as to other regions. While the evidence is inconclusive, studies from IPEA in Brazil suggest that so far Brazil has failed to do so (Fernanda de Negri, 2005). The mega contracts won in 2006 by Embraer, the jet producer (100 jet sales to China), might help to change this pattern. Research has also been conducted on employment showing that trade with China and India had only a small negative effect on industrial employment (see for Argentina Castro, Olarreaga, and Saslavsky, 2006).

China and Latin America have intensively developed their trade relations over the past decade[36]. Trade volume rose from $2 billion in the early 1990s to $15 billion in 2001, according to Chinese statistics. Since 2000, Brazilian-Chinese trade has leapt nearly threefold, a blessing for the indebted Brazilian economy and especially for exporters of soybeans, steel and iron ore, which accounted for two-thirds of the goods exported. In general, Latin America has a commodity endowment that boosts synergies with China's needs and its strategy to secure food and energy imports in order to avoid shortages.

One consequence of China's booming demand on Latin America might not be as positive, however. With increasing Chinese commodities demand, Latin American countries are deepening their trade specialisation toward commodities that have been characterised traditionally by strong price volatility (Devlin *et al.*, 2006; Gottschalk and Prates, 2005). Such exposure could also increase the volatility of fiscal receipts. Moreover, with the intensification of its links with China, the region is becoming more exposed to the Asian economy. In 2003 delivery bottlenecks and demand from China pumped up prices of raw materials and commodities. Chinese industrial use of them is susceptible to swings due to recessions and booms. The growing Chinese dependence on Latin American exports also requires the area to be more aware of growth dynamics in Asia and China. In 2003, China became the second largest destination for Brazilian exports according to ECLAC (CEPAL, 2004). In 2004, China accounted for half the increase in Brazil's export earnings. China is therefore becoming a key driver of Brazilian growth dynamics, accounting for one-fourth of Brazil's officially targeted GDP growth. With China trying to cool down its overheated economy, Brazil's export growth could dampen.

An issue that deserves further analysis involves capital flows. While FDI to Latin America has been tumbling during the early 2000s, FDI towards China soared. Between 2001 and 2003, FDI into Mexico declined from nearly $27 billion to $11 billion – later it recovered in 2004, 2005 and 2006. Brazil also experienced an abrupt drop of 52 per cent in FDI between 2002 and 2003 (*versus* -30 per cent for Mexico). Meanwhile, China became the world's major FDI recipient with an inflow of $55 billion in 2003, nearly twice the total flow of $36.5 billion to all of Latin America that year[37]. The Chinese inflow reached around $60 billion 2004 and in 2005 – i.e. more than $1 billion per week over the past three years (in 2006, they reached $63 billion)[38]. It is true that much FDI to China, estimated at one-fourth of total inflows, is in fact related to round-tripping (Xiao, 2005). FDI from other areas is increasing, however. By 2002, US firms were already investing ten times more in China than a decade before. The prospect of a huge domestic market of 1.3 billion consumers has lured countless companies to rush into China, despite the fact that the country's capitalism is not solidly rooted in law, protection of property rights and free markets[39].

Some studies already suggest "flow diversion" in favour of China in the process of full integration of China's huge labour force into the international division of labour[40]. Asian countries like Indonesia, Malaysia, the Philippines and Thailand might suffer significant welfare losses if FDI is redirected away from them to China. They risk de-industrialisation and a return to their roles in the 1950s and 1960s as primary-commodity exporters (McKibbin and Thye Woo, 2004). Both studies and the data show that this impact is rather small for Latin America, however. For the long period from 1984 to 2001, García-Herrero and Santabárbara (2004; and one of the following chapters in this book) find no substitution effect from Latin American inward FDI to China, although they do underline that the Chinese effect became more significant towards the end of the period (1995-2001). Chinese inward FDI appears to have hampered FDI to Mexico and Colombia especially. As we have seen, the data for 2004 and 2005 are mixed, suggesting that, while China still had an FDI boom, Latin American countries were recovering from earlier floor levels. FDI in Brazil jumped by 80 per cent in 2004 to reach more than $18 billion.

Mexico had a recovery of 23 per cent to $13.6 billion in 2004, and Chile saw its FDI increase by 66 per cent to nearly $5 billion. The 2006 data confirmed a seemingly booming trend: Mexico lured $20 billion of FDI, a level on the rise when compared to the already very good year of 2005 ($17.8 billion) The golden years of the FDI rush to Latin America in the 1990s might be over, at least until the processes of privatisation are reopened, but FDI is still flowing to Latin America.

The future development of Chinese foreign investment overseas may be a blessing in disguise. China is no longer only an FDI absorber; its foreign FDI has made a forward leap. Over the whole 1991-2003 period, cumulative outward Chinese FDI reached roughly $35 billion. In 2003 alone, the annual outflow more than doubled to above $2 billion and reached in 2005 a record of $7billion (for an analysis of the implications of Chinese buy outs in developed and developing countries see Antkiewicz and Whalley, 2006). In 2006, FDI from China reached $16.1 billion according to official statistics. The need to secure food and commodities resources is boosting FDI through strategic international partnerships. Chinese firms have already targeted resource-sector investments in Angola, Algeria, Australia and Indonesia. Chinese companies are prominent investors in Africa, mainly in energy and raw materials. According to a survey of 100 investment-promotion agencies released by UNCTAD, China ranked fifth after the United States, Germany, the United Kingdom and France as one of the leading overseas investors in the near future (UNCTAD, 2004). In 2004 and 2005, Chinese corporations multiplied attempts to boost their investments overseas, not only in other emerging countries, but also in developed ones – as underlined by Lenovo's acquisition of IBM production units (for $1.75 billion), attempts by Chinese firms such as Minmetals to acquire the Canadian Noranda for $5 billion or the Chinese oil group CNOOC's bid to acquire the US Unocal for more than $13 billion. They are not alone in this game; India is also emerging as a rising investor overseas. In 2006-2007, Indian companies would have invested more than $11 billion outside India, had the take over of steelmaker Corus by the Indian giant Tata gone through, almost double the amount of inbound FDI over the same period. Colombia, Brazil and Bolivia, have been some of the major destinations of these investments abroad (see for a comparison between India and China's presences in Latin America and Africa, Goldstein, Pinaud, Reisen and Chen, 2006; Deutsche Bank Research, 2006; Zhang, 2006; Santiso, 2006).

Like the Japanese a few decades ago, Chinese firms seem to be looking for overseas expansion. This looks like an opportunity for Latin America. Not only are two big Asian countries, Japan and China, interested in the area, but both seek the same thing, i.e. to secure a continuous flow of raw materials and agricultural products. To reach that goal, both have interests in reliable infrastructure in the Americas, including more efficient ports, roads and railways. This gives the region a unique opportunity to play a new competitive game. It encourages more thinking in terms of industrial strategies to avoid a re-deepening of commodity-trade specialisation and to stimulate (as in Trinidad and Tobago, for example) diversification towards more value-added industries, building on the commodity endowment.

Latin America seems to be on the radars of Chinese companies. By 2001, China had set up more than 300 enterprises in Latin America with contractual investments of over $1 billion. In 2004, half of Chinese FDI went to Latin America, exceeding the 30 per cent that went to Asia (in 2005 16 per cent of a total record of $7 billion went to Latin America). During the 2000s companies like Baosteel, China's biggest steelmaker, undertook China's hitherto biggest-ever overseas foreign direct investment ($1.5 billion) in Brazil. China also announced plans to invest $2 billion in the Brazilian aluminium industry. China already controls Peru's major iron-ore mine, through Shougang Group; it owns a major stake in an Ecuadorian oil field; and it is trying to produce fuel and to reactivate gold mines in Venezuela. Chinese investment is expected in railways and ports in Brazil and generally throughout Latin America, because Chinese interest in logistical infrastructure is high in order to facilitate the transport of commodities to ports. In Argentina, China is already committed to invest $25 million in a grain port and another $250 million in a road from Argentina to Chile for the export of Argentine raw materials from Chilean ports. The agreements between Chinese and Latin American companies exploded. The Chinese state oil company Sinopec, for example, invested $1 billion in a joint venture with Petrobras for the construction of a gas pipeline linking south to northeast Brazil. Other deals the Chinese have recently signed included iron ore shipments from Companhia Vale do Rio Doce (CVRD), one of the world's largest mining concerns, for Shanghai's famous Baoshan Steel Mill. In 2005, Codelco, the Chilean copper giant signed an historical trade contract with Chinese Minmetals.

The region also started to witness agreements such as that signed in October 2004 by Telefónica, the leading Spanish firm with a regional Latin American franchise, and the giant Chinese telecommunication equipment maker Huawei; Telefónica offered Huawei facilities to enter the Latin American market in a move to sell products for all of Telefónica's Latin American subsidiaries[41].

Latin American companies also seek business opportunities in China, as evidenced by the official trip to China by the Brazilian President Lula and nearly 400 Brazilian businessmen in 2004. Some large Latin American companies have already rushed to China, such as Embraer, a Brazilian aircraft-maker that sells and produces jets in China (for a case study see Goldstein, 2004) or Marcopolo, another Brazilian company, which makes bus chassis and is planning to set up a Chinese factory. Clearly, capital flows between China and Latin America deserve more analysis and invite further research, expanding on Chapter 1 of this volume.

Beyond the trade and investment impacts, there is perhaps a third and last Chinese impact: a cognitive effect (Santiso, 2006). China's very pragmatic economic development strategy attracts more and more attention. Leading economists like Ricardo Hausmann and Dani Rodrik have already emphasised the trade dimension of this unusual emerging giant, the Chinese economic miracle being a matter not only of export volumes but also and above all of their increasing quality (Rodrik, 2006; Hausmann *et al.*, 2006; Rodrik and Hausmann, 2006). The very pragmatic economic approach of the Chinese authorities is also catching the attention of policy makers around the world. The Chinese miracle is neither the result of some miracle driven by the Chicago Boys nor the output of a Kemmerer mission. No foreign advisor or economic development guru ever landed in China. If Jeffrey Sachs advised Bolivia, he never reached Beijing, at least with his advice. Another lesson from China teaches that there is no magic formula for development, no magical key to a unique paradigm that will open the doors of the miracle of development.

Notes

1. The authors are indebted to Santiago Sanz, Juan Antonio Rodríguez and Luciana Taft for their technical support and useful comments. They are also grateful to José María Álvarez Pallete, Claustre Bajona, Jean Christophe Bas, Dominique Bocquet, Guillermo Calvo, Eliana Cardoso, Luis Miguel Castilla, Carlos Elizondo, Barry Eichengreen, Antoni Estevadeordal, Albert Fishlow, Ernesto Gaba, Alicia García-Herrero, Andrea Goldstein, Ricardo Hausmann, Bert Hofman, Louka Katseli, Nathaniel Karp, Sanjay Lall, Richard Lapper, Nicholas Lardy, Bénédicte Larre, Eduardo Lora, Ya Lan Liu, Osmel Manzano, Diane McCollum, Alejandro Micco, Charles Oman, Luisa Palacios, Mixin Pei, Guillermo Perry, Nicolas Pinaud, Helmut Reisen, Germán Ríos, Dani Rodrik, Manuel Sánchez, David Taguas, for helpful documentations, suggestions and discussions. This chapter draws heavily on the OECD Development Centre Working Paper No. 252 (Blázquez, Rodríguez and Santiso, 2006); and on an earlier version in ECLAC Review (December, 2006).

2. Respectively Advisor in the Economic Bureau of Presidency of Spanish Government (formerly, while conducting this research, Senior Economist at BBVA Research Department), Chief Development Economist and Deputy Director of the OECD Development Centre (previously Chief Economist for Latin America and Emerging Markets at BBVA Research Department) and Economist at BBVA. E-Mail: javier.santiso@oecd.org. Paper presented at the Centre for Latin American Studies of Georgetown University, Washington, D.C., 4 October 2004; at the Institute for Latin American Studies of Columbia University, New York, October 6th 2004; at the conference co-organized by The World Bank and Deutsche Bank, "Asia and Latin America: Opportunities and Challenges - The World Bank Ninth LAC Meets the Market Conference", New York, 26 October 2004; at the 9th LACEA Meeting, San José, Costa Rica, 4-6 November 2004; at the *Corporación Andina de Fomento*, Caracas, 1 December 2004; at the OECD Development Centre, Paris, 21 January 2005; at the Inter-American Development Bank 2005 Annual Meeting, Official Seminar on "Latin America and Asia in the world economy: Towards more interregional economic linkages and cooperation", Okinawa, 8 April 2005; at the Annual Bank Conference on Development Economics – Europe organised by The World Bank, Amsterdam, 23-24 May 2005; and at the Annual Bank Conference on Development Economics – Europe organised by The World Bank, Tokyo, 29 May-2 June 2006.

3. Uncertainties about Chinese statistics abound. In 2003, for example, the official GDP growth rate was 9.1 per cent, but almost all economists following China suspected that figure was over 11 per cent. On the contrary, Alwyn Young (2003) estimated that GDP growth over 1978-1998 was 1.7 percentage points below the official rate.

4. China is the second-largest economy, valued at Power Purchasing Parity (PPP), after the United States.

5. Goldman Sachs has had an aggressive strategy to enter China. This US-based global investment bank runs its business in the Asia-Pacific region with an office in Hong Kong as headquarters. Goldman Sachs also has offices in Beijing and Shanghai for China business contacts. In Asia it employs over 1 000 people and 150 of them deal with Chinese businesses. See Yao *et al.* (2003).

6. Worries about the Chinese currency intensified during 2003-04, the latter an electoral year in the United States (Eichengreen, 2004; Eichengren, March 2006).

7. On the Chinese banking system, see Deutsche Bank (2004) and Banco de España (2004). Over the past two decades the rush of foreign banks into the Chinese financial system has intensified, reflecting the deeper trade relations between China and the world. HSBC, Citgroup, Scotia, Crédit Lyonnais and BNP Paribas are among the foreign commercial banks with the greatest representation. Among the investment bankers, the most active are Goldman Sachs, Morgan Stanley, Deutsche Bank, JP Morgan, UBS and CSFB. In 2003, investment banks shared more than $200 million in fees (not enough to cover their costs) for IPOs of China-based companies according to estimates by *Dealogic* reported in the *Financial Times*.

8. See Maddison (1998) for a historical perspective on the Chinese economy and Shiue and Keller (2004, February and September).

9. See LAEBA web site: http://www.laeba.org/index.cfm

10. On this performance and its sustainability, see Yifu Lin (2004) and Zijian Wang and Wei (2004).

11. One indicator of the increasing competitive tensions generated by the emergence of China is the increase in anti-dumping investigations against China. China has become the top anti-dumping target (Chua and Prusa, 2004).

12. For example, the poor performance of the industrial sector in the United States, despite its significant growth during 2002-2004, is attributed indirectly to China. There is an "off-shoring" process in which US corporations transfer their manufacturing activities to China due to its low labour costs. For the same reason, some analysts claim that the poor performance of Mexican exports in recent years is due to China.

13. This database can be found on line at www.intracen.org.

14. See, for example, "El Ataque del Dragón" ("The Attack of the Dragon"), (26 December 2003), *America Economia.com* (www.americaeconomia.com) and "Challenges from China Spur Mexican Factories to Elevate Aspirations", (5 March 2004), *Wall Street Journal*.

15. The correlation between both indexes is 0.94. This shows that both indexes report the same information.

16. In May 2004, Brazilian President Luiz Inacio Lula da Silva took more than 400 executives with him to China, the biggest Brazilian official delegation ever to make a trade trip.

17. Soler (2003) reaches the same conclusion: China jeopardises Mexican exports; but the final impact on Mexico depends not only on trade competition, but also on the evolution of capital flows.

18. For other countries see Appendix 1.

19. The source is BBVA database.

20. This information is available on line at www.intracen.org.

21. In this sense, the Panamá-Puebla highway – a new infrastructure project – could generate a significant increase of trade among Central American countries, Mexico and the United States.

22. They also show that distance matters and that it has a significant (1 per cent) positive effect on transport costs; a doubling in distance generates roughly an 18 per cent increase in transport costs. See the table in Appendix 2.

23. Limao and Venables (2000) showed that raising transport costs by 10 per cent reduces trade volumes by more than 20 per cent. They also underlined that poor infrastructure accounts for more than 40 per cent of the predicted transport costs.

24. China imports chemical products mainly from East Asian countries, however. This sector is one in which those Asian economies are specialised. See Ianchovichina and Walmsley (2003).

25. In 2002 China took 23.2 per cent of world imports of soybeans as against only 7.4 per cent in 1997. For copper the shares were 16.8 per cent in 2002 and 5 per cent in 1997. For oil they were 4.2 per cent and 2.3 per cent respectively.

26. See, for example, *Análisis Macroeconómico y Financiero* (2003). This issue analyses the benefits for Argentina of trade with China.

27. On the Asian oil market, see also the study carried out by the Honolulu based east-West Centre: http://www.eastwestcenter.org/stored/pdfs/api070.pdf

28. See, for instance, IMF (2004). This issue also analyses the emergence of East Asia.

29. This comparison is suggested by Yang (2003).

30. This chapter defines trade as the sum of exports and imports.
31. The source is the Summers and Heston database (PWT 6.1). See Heston and Summers (1997).
32. Net exports are defined as the difference between exports and imports in real terms.
33. Ianchovichina and Martin (2001) share this opinion about the future of net exports. They expect a significant increase in China's imports.
34. The GDP per capita is calculated in PPP terms.
35. IMF database.
36. Initial trade contacts between China and Latin America are far from new. They date back to the 1570s, when sino-Latin American trade started to flourish across the Pacific with Chinese exports of silk, porcelain and cotton yarn to Mexico and Peru *via* Manila. See Shixue, 2004.
37. See ECLAC (2004) report on FDI in Latin America: http://www.eclac.cl/. The 2003 FDI flows to China in fact reached nearly the record level of Latin American FDI inflows ($88 billion in 1999).
38. On FDI in China see the research of MIT based economist Huang, http://web.mit.edu/yshuang/www/publications/papers.html. See also US Congressional hearing, http://www.cecc.gov/pages/hearings/092403/huang.php
39. Investing in China might become a risky business, however, as underlined by growing disputes between foreigners and their Chinese partners. In 2004, for example, Syngenta, a Swiss agrichemicals company, sued a Chinese competitor for allegedly pirating one of its patented insecticides, joining the growing club of foreign investors resorting to the courts to protect their intellectual property. The profitability of Chinese investments can also be questionable. Foreign brewers, for example, have squandered hundreds of millions of dollars in China over the past decade. The average net profit margin of these investments is meagre: for the top 400 brewers operating in China (including foreign joint ventures) it is just 0.5 per cent. Compared with Latin America the profitability data are interesting. Direct and indirect profits made by all American affiliates operating in China amounted to just $2.8 billion in 2001, about half as much as the $4.4 billion dollars made the same year in Mexico (with a population less than one-tenth as large). According to empirical studies of political control and firm performance in China's listed companies, the decision-making power of local party committees (relative to the largest shareholders) is positively associated with firm performance (Chang and Wong, 2003; Wong *et al.*, 2004).
40. For empirical analysis applied to Latin America see García-Herrero and Santabárbara (2004) and Chantasassawat *et al.* (2004). For analysis focused on Asia see Eichengreen and Tong, (May 2005 and December 2005) and Mercereau (2005).

41. Huawei is a clear example of the internationalisation of Chinese companies. The company hopes to increase its international sales from $2.3 billion in 2004 to more than $10 billion by 2008 as part of an ambitious global expansion strategy. In 2003, Huawei contracted 27 per cent of its $4 billion in sales outside China, reaching markets such as Sweden and the Netherlands. The company is now present in more than 70 countries and over 3 000 of the group's 24 000 employees are based overseas. In 2004, two-fifths of its $5 billion in revenues were generated outside China (*The Economist*, 8 January 2005; *Financial Times*, 11 January 2005). However Yasheng Huang underlines (*Financial Times*, 14 January 2005, p.13), most of the "Chinese champions" are in fact foreign companies. Lenovo, the purchaser in 2004 of IBM's personal computer business, is a clear example. Technically speaking it is a foreign company because it organised its operations in China as subsidiaries of its Hong Kong arm. The four Chinese companies listed in Forbes as the most dynamic all have their headquarters in Hong Kong. As Huang stresses, it seems that "China's success has less to do with creating efficient institutions and more about allowing such an escape from inefficient institutions." See also http://web.mit.edu/yshuang/www/

Bibliography

AHEARNE, A., J. FERNALD, P. LOUNGANI AND J. SCHINDLER (2003), "China and Emerging Asia: Comrades or Competitors?", International Finance Discussion Paper, No. 789, Board of Governors, Federal Reserve System, Washington, D.C., December.

America Economia.com, "El Ataque del Dragón", 26 December 2003.

Análisis Macroeconómico y Financiero (2003), Departamento de Research del BBVA Banco Frances.

Análisis Macroeconómico y Financiero (2004), Departamento de Research del BBVA Banco Frances, February.

ANDERSON, J. AND E. VAN WINCOOP (2003), "Gravity with Gravitas: A Solution to the Border Puzzle", *American Economic Review*, 93, pp. 170-192.

ANDERSON, J. AND E. VAN WINCOOP (2004), "Trade Costs", *Journal of Economic Literature*, 42(3), pp. 691-751, September. See: http://fmwww.bc.edu/ec-p/wp593.pdf

ANTKIEWICZ, A. AND J WHALLEY (2006), "Recent Chinese Buyout Activity and its Implications for Global Architecture", NBER Working Paper, 12072, March.

BANCO DE ESPAÑA (2004), "Where is the Chinese banking sector going? Banking reform in the People's Republic of China", *Banco de España, Asuntos Internationales* (unpublished), April.

BERGES, R. (2004), "Implications of Eventual Changes to China's Peg", *Latin America Investment Strategy Implications*, Merrill Lynch, March.

BERTHELON, M. AND C. FREUND (2003), "On the Conservation of Distance in International Trade", University of Maryland and The World Bank (unpublished conference paper), November.

BLÁZQUEZ, J. AND J. SANTISO (2004), "China: ¿Angel or demonio para América latina?", *Economía Exterior*, 30, pp. 123-132, Autumn.

BLÁZQUEZ, J., J. RODRÍGUEZ AND J. SANTISO (2006), "Angel or Devil? China's Trade Impact on Latin American Emerging Markets", *Working Paper* No. 252, OECD Development Centre, June.

BRUN, J.F., C. CARRÈRE, P. GUILLAUMONT AND J. DE MELO (2005), "Has Distance Died ? Evidence from A Gravity Model", *World Bank Economic Review* (forthcoming).

BUSSIERE, M. AND B. SCHNATZ (2006), "Evaluation China's Integration in World Trade with a Gravity Model Based Bechmark", *European Central Bank, Working Paper Series*, 693, November.

CAF (2006), *América latina en el comercio global. Ganando mercados*, CAF, Caracas.

CARRÈRE, C. AND M. SCHIFF (2003), "On the geography of trade: distance is alive and well", *CERDI Université d'Auvergne and The World Bank* (unpublished), December. See: http://team.univ-paris1.fr/teamperso/disdier/meta.pdf

CASTRO, L., C. TRAMUTOLA AND P. MONAT (2005) *China, como puede la Argentina aprovechar la gran oportunidad*. Buenos Aires, Editorial Edhasa.

CASTRO, L., M. OLARREAGA AND D. SASLAVSKY (2006), "The Impact of Trade with China and India on Argentina's Manufacturing Employement", mimeo unpublished, available at http://mpra.ub.uni-muenchen.de/538/01/MPRA_paper_538.pdf, August.

CERA – CAMBRIDGE ENERGY RESEARCH ASSOCIATES (2004), *Riding the Tiger: The global impact of China's energy quandary*, CERA, Cambridge, MA.

CEPAL (2004), "Los efectos de la adhesión de China a la OMC en las relaciones económicas con América Latina y el Caribe", in CEPAL, *Panorama de la inserción internacional de América Latina y el Caribe, 2002-2003* Chapter VI, CEPAL, Santiago de Chile.

CHANG, E. AND S. WONG (2003), "Political Control and Performance in China's Listed Companies", The University of Hong Kong, Faculty of Business and Economics (unpublished), March.

CHANTASASAWAT, B., K.C. FUNG, H. IIZAKA AND A. SIU (2004), "Foreign Direct Investment in East Asia and Latin America: Is there a People's Republic of China Effect?", ADB Institute Discussion Paper, No. 17.

CHONG-EN BAI, CHANG-TAI HSIEH, YINGYI QIAN (2006), "The Return to Capital in China", *NBER Working Paper*, 12755, December.

CHU, T. AND T. PRUSA (2004), "The Reasons for and the Impact of Anti-dumping Protection: The Case of People's Republic of China", *East-West Centre Working Papers*, No. 69, April. See http://www.eastwestcenter.org/stored/pdfs/ECONwp069.pdf

CLARK, X., D. DOLLAR AND A. MICCO (2004), "Port Efficiency, Maritime Transport Costs and Bilateral Trade", *Journal of Development Economics*, Vol. 75, No. 2, pp. 417-450, December.

DEARDORFF, A. (2004), "Local Comparative Advantage: Trade Costs and the Pattern of Trade", University of Michigan Gerald Ford School of Public Policy, Discussion Paper, No. 500, February. See the web site: http://www.fordschool.umich.edu/rsie/workingpapers/Papers476-500/r500.pdf

DE NEGRI, F. (2005), "O perfil dos exportadores industriais brasileirospara a China", *IPEA Texto para Discussaô*, 1091 . See http://www.ipea.gov.br/pub/td/2005/td_1091.pdf

DEVLIN, R., A. ESTEVADEORDAL AND A. RODRÍGUEZ-CLARE (2006), *The Emergence of China*, Washington, D.C., IDB.

DEUTSCHE BANK RESEARCH (2006), *China's Commodity Hunger: Implication for Africa and Latin America*, Deutsche Bank Research, Frankfurt, June.

DEUTSCHE BANK RESEARCH (2004), *China's financial sector: institutional framework and main challenges,*, Deutsche Bank Research, Frankfurt, January.

DISDIER, A.C. AND K. HEAD (2004), "Exaggerated Reports of the Death of Distance: Lessons from a Meta-Analysis", *Paris I Panthéon La Sorbonne and University of British Columbia* (unpublished), January. See: http://team.univ-paris1.fr/teamperso/disdier/meta.pdf

DOMÍNGUEZ, J. (2006), "China's Relations with Latin America: Shared Gains, Asymmetric Hopes", *Inter-American Dialogue Working Paper*, available at http://www.thedialogue.org/publications/2006/summer/china.pdf, June.

ECLAC (ECONOMIC COMMISSION FOR LATIN AMERICA AND THE CARIBBEAN) (2004), *Report on Foreign Direct Investment (FDI) in Latin America*, http://www.eclac.cl/.

EICHENGREEN, B. (2004), "Chinese Currency Controversies," Paper presented for Economic Panel, Hong Kong, April.

EICHENGREEN, B. (2006), "China's Exchange Rate Regime: The Long and Short of It", University of California at Berkeley, Economics Department (unpublished), March.

EICHENGREEN, B. AND H. TONG (2005), "Is China's FDI Coming at the Expense of other Countries?", National Bureau of Economic Research, Working Paper 11335, May.

EICHENGREEN, B. AND H. TONG (2005), "How China Is Reorganizing the World Economy", University of California at Berkeley, Economics Department, and Bank of England (unpublished), December.

EICHENGREEN, B., Y. RHEE AND H. TONG (2004), "The Impact of China on the Exports of other Asian Countries", National Bureau of Economic Research, Working Paper No. 10768, September.

EVANS, C. AND J. HARRIGAN (2003), "Distance, Time, and Specialization", National Bureau of Economic Research, Working Paper, No. 9729, May. See also http://www.ny.frb.org/research/economists/harrigan/papers.html

Financial Times, 11 January 2005, "The Challenge from China: Why Huawei Is Making the Telecoms World Take Notice", p. 11.

GARCÍA-HERRERO, A. AND D. SANTABÁRBARA (2004), "Does China have an impact on Foreign Direct Investment to Latin America?", Banco de España, working paper presented at the First LAEBA Conference on the Challenges and Opportunities of the Emergence of China, Beijing, December.

GLAESER, E. AND J. KOHLHASE (2003), "Cities, Regions and the Decline of Transportation Costs", Harvard Institute of Economic Research, Discussion Paper, No. 2014, July. See also: http://post.economics.harvard.edu/hier/2003papers/HIER2014.pdf

GOLDSTEIN, A. (2004), "A Latin American Global Player Goes to Asia: Embraer in China", OECD Development Centre, mimeo (unpublished).

GOLDSTEIN, A., N. PINAUD, H. REISEN AND X. CHEN (2006), *The Rise of China and India: What's In It for Africa?*, OECD Development Centre Study, París.

GOTTSCHALK, R. AND D. PRATES (2005), "The Macroeconomic Challenges of East Asia's Growing Demand for Primary Commodities in Latin America", *Institute of Development Studies, Working Paper*, available at http://www.ids.ac.uk/ids/global/pdfs/RGMacro%20Challenge.pdf

HANSON, G. AND R. ROBERTSON, (2006), "China and the Recent Evolution of Mexico's Manufacturing Exports", University of California, San Diego, Working Paper; can be downloadable at http://irpshome.ucsd.edu/faculty/gohanson/working_papers.htm, June.

HARRIGAN, J. AND A. VENABLES (2004), "Timeliness, Trade and Agglomeration", National Bureau of Economic Research, Working Paper No. 10404, March.

HAUSMANN, R., J. HWANG AND D. RODRIK (2006), "What You Export Matters", Harvard University, John F. Kennedy School of Government and Department of Economics, March (unpublished), March.

HAUSMANN, R., E. LIM AND M. SPENCE (2006), "China and the Global Economy: Medium-term issues and options – a synthesis report", *Harvard University, Kennedy School of Government, Working Paper*, 29, July.

HAUSMANN, R. AND D. RODRIK (2006), "Doomed to Choose: Industrial Policy as Predicament", *Harvard University, Kennedy School of Government* (unpublished), September.

HESTON, A. AND R. SUMMERS (1997), "PPPs and Price Parities in Benchmark Studies and the Penn World Table", *CICUP 97-1*, paper presented at a Eurostat conference.

HUANG, Y. (2003), *Selling China*, Cambridge University Press, Cambridge, MA.

HUANG. Y. (2005), "China's Big Hope is Not Hong-Kong", *Financial Times*, 14 January, p. 13.

HUMMELS, D. (2001*a*), "Toward A Geography of Trade Costs", Purdue University, Krannert School of Management (unpublished), September. See http://www.mgmt.purdue.edu/faculty/hummelsd/

HUMMELS, D. (2001b). "Time as A Trade Barrier", Purdue University, Krannert School of Management (unpublished), July. See http://www.mgmt.purdue.edu/faculty/hummelsd/ Washington, D.C.

IANCHOVICHINA, E. AND W. MARTIN (2001), "Trade Liberalization in China's Accession to the World Trade Organization", The World Bank, Washington DC (unpublished).

IANCHOVICHINA, E. AND W. MARTIN (2003), "Economic Impacts of China's Accession to the World Trade Organization", World Bank Policy Research Working Paper 3053.

IANCHOVICHINA, E. AND T. WALMSLEY (2003), "Impact of China's WTO Accession on East Asia", World Bank Policy Research Working Paper 3109, Washington, D.C.

INTER-AMERICAN DEVELOPMENT BANK (IDB) (2004). "The emergence of China: Opportunities and challenges for Latin America and the Caribbean", paper prepared for discussion at the conference on "The Emergence of China: Opportunities and Challenges for Latin America and the Caribbean", Washington, D.C., 1 October.

INTER-AMERICAN DEVELOPMENT BANK (IDB) (2006), *The Emergence of China*, Washington, DC, IDB.

INTERNATIONAL MONETARY FUND (IMF) (2004), "Chapter II: The Global Implications of the US Fiscal Deficit and of China's Growth", in *World Economic Outlook*, IMF, Washington, D.C.

LALL, S. AND J. WEISS (2004). "People's Republic of China Competitive Threat to Latin America: An Analysis for 1990-2002", Asian Development Bank Institute Discussion Paper, No. 14 (unpublished), October, Manila.

LANE, P. AND S. SCHMUKLER (AUGUST 2006), "The International Financial Integration of China and India", *Institute for International Integration Studies, IIS Discussion Paper*, 174.

Latinwatch, June 2003 and April 2004, Banco Bilbao Vizcaya Argentaria (BBVA), Madrid.

LEDERMAN, D., M.OLARREAGA, AND G.PERRY (2006), "Latin America and the Caribbean's Response to the Growth of China and India: Overview of Research Findings and Policy Implications", Office of the Chief Economist for Latin America and The Caribbean at The World Bank, paper prepared for the *Program of Seminars at the World Bank and IMF Annual Meetings* held in Singapore, August.

LEDERMAN, D., M.OLARREAGA, AND E. RUBIANO (2006), "Latin America's Trade Specialization and China and India's Growth", *The World Bank* (mimeo unpublished).

LIMAO, N. AND A.J. VENABLES (2000), "Infrastructure, Geographical Disadvantage and Transport Costs", *The World Bank Economic Review*, vol. 15, n° 3, pp. 451-479.

LIN, J. (2004), "The People's Republic of China: Future Development and Economic Relations with Latin America" (unpublished) Asian Development Bank Institute, Manila, November.

LORA, E. (2004*a*), "Es posible competir con la China ? Fortalezas y debilidades de China respecto a América Latina", *IDB Research Department* (unpublished), Washington DC, April.

LORA, E. (2004*b*), "Can Latin America Compete with China?", IDB Research Department (PowerPoint presentation), April.

MADDISON, A. (1998), *Chinese Economic Performance in the Long Run*, OECD Development Centre Studies, Paris.

MCKIBBIN, W. AND W. THYE WOO (2004). "The Consequences of China's WTO Accession on its Neighbors", Brookings Discussion Papers in International Economics, No. 157 and *Asian Economic Papers*.

MERCEREAU, B. (2005), "FDI Flows to Asia: Did the Dragon Crowd out the Tigers?", IMF Working Paper, No. 189, Washington, D.C, September.

PAIVA DE ABREU, M. DE (2005). "China's emergence in the global economy and Brazil", *PUC Rio, Economic Department*, 491 (unpublished), January.

RODRIK, D. (2006), "What's So Special about China's Exports?", Harvard University, John F. Kennedy School of Government (unpublished), January.

RUMBAUGH, T. AND N. BLANCHER (2004), "China: International Trade and WTO Accession", International Monetary Fund Working Paper WP/04/36, March.

SAEED QRESHI, M. AND G. WAN (2006), "Trade Potential of China and India: Threat or Opportunity?", *Trinity College, University of Cambridge and United Nations University, World Institute for Development Economics Research*, May available at http://siteresources.worldbank.org/INTDECABCTOK2006/Resources/UNU-Wider_2-2.pdf

SANTISO, J. (2006), "¿Realisno mágico? China e India en América latina y en África", *Economía Exterior*, 38, pp. 59-69.

SANTISO, J. AND A. NEUT (2006), "India y Brasil: El Elefante y el tucán", *Economía Exterior*, 39, pp. 107-114

SHIUE, C. AND W. KELLER (2004), "Market Integration and Economic Development: A Long-run Comparison", National Bureau of Economic Research Working Paper No. 10300, February.

SHIUE, C. AND W. KELLER (2004). "Markets in China and Europe on the Eve of the Industrial Revolution", National Bureau of Economic Research Working Paper No. 10778, September.

SHIXUE, J. (2004), "Sino-Latin America Economic Relations and China's Perspective on Latin American Economy", Institute of Latin American Studies, Chinese Academy of Social Sciences, Beijing, China (unpublished).

SOLER, J. (2003), "Impacto Sobre los Flujos Comerciales entre China y el Mundo", in J. SOLER (eds.) *El despertar de la nueva China. Implicaciones del ingreso de China en la Organización Mundial del Comercio* pp. 53-73. Los Libros de la Catarata (Cyan), Madrid.

The Economist, 8 January 2005, "Special Report: China's Champions", pp. 58-59.

UNCTAD (2004), *Prospects for FDI flows, Transnational Corporations' Strategies and Promotion Policies: 2004-2007*, Global investment prospects assessment (GIPA) research note 1: results of a survey of location experts, UNCTAD, Geneva, April.

XIAO, G. (2005), "Round-tripping Foreign Direct Investment in the People's Republic of China: Scale, Causes, and Implications", *Asian Development Bank Institute, ADBI Policy Research Brief*, No.10, ADB, Manila, January.

YANG, Y. (2003), "China's Integration into the World Economy: Implications for Developing Countries", International Monetary Fund Working Paper WP/03/245, IMF, Washington, D.C.

YAO, Y., F. LI, E. TOLAN, I. ISKENDEROV AND S. DHAR (2003), "Goldman Sachs' China Challenges", Norwegian School of Economics MIB Paper (unpublished), Oslo.

YIFU LIN, J. (2004), "Is China's Growth Real and Sustainable?", China Centre for Economic Research, Peking University, Working Paper No. 2004-2 (unpublished). See http://www.ccer.pku.edu.cn/download/3024-1.pdf.

YOUNG, A. (2003), "Gold into Base Metals: Productivity growth in the People's Republic of China during the Reform period", *Journal of Political Economy*, vol. 111, n° 6, December, pp. 1220-1261.

Wall Street Journal, 5 March 2004, "Challenges from China Spur Mexican Factories to Elevate Aspirations".

WONG, S., S. OPPER AND R. HU (2004), "Shareholding Structure, Depoliticization, and Firm Performance: Lessons from China's Listed Firms", *Economic Transition*, Vol. 12 (1), pp.29-66.

ZHANG, Z. (SEPTEMBER 2006), "China's Hunt for Oil in Africa in Perspective", *East West Centre, Research Program* (unpublished).

ZIJIAN WANG, S. AND J. WEI (2004), "Structural Change, Capital's Contribution, and Economic Efficiency: Sources of China's Economic Growth Between 1952-1998", Göteborg University – Department of Economics Working Paper (unpublished).

ISBN: 9789264027961

Chapter Three

China and Latin America: Trade Competition, 1990-2002

by Sanjaya Lall and John Weiss[1]

Abstract

This chapter explores the competitive threat posed by People's Republic of China (PRC) to the Latin America and Caribbean region (LAC). It focuses on the impact of the PRC's rise as a major exporter of manufactures, and examines these issues with trade data for 1990-2002 (at the time of writing 2003 data were not available for all relevant countries), analysing and comparing export performance and specialisation patterns in the world as a whole and in the United States, the main market for both the PRC and LAC.

The explosive growth of Chinese exports over the past decade has led to much discussion of its competitive threat in developed as well as developing countries. At the popular level, the threat seems quite clear. Between 1990 and 2002, the PRC's manufactured exports grew by 16.6 per cent per annum, from $48 billion to $303.5 billion[2], raising China's world market share over three-fold from 1.9 per cent to 6.4 per cent. In 2002, the PRC overtook the United Kingdom and in 2003 it overtook France, becoming the fourth largest exporter in the world after the United States, Germany and Japan. In the developing world it was by far the largest exporter; its share of manufactured exports more than doubled (in a faster-growing total), from 11.3 per cent to 24.1 per cent.

ISBN: 9789264027961

In response to falling trade costs and greater international capital mobility the PRC has emerged as a major exporter at both the labour-intensive, low-technology end of the product spectrum and increasingly at the knowledge-intensive, higher-technology end. For the former, the large labour surplus in rural China has ensured a plentiful labour supply for the export sector at what has been a relatively constant real wage set by the low opportunity cost of rural labour. In consequence, in a wide range of activities the PRC has been the marginal supplier of low-technology goods to the world market, and its productivity and wage level have set world prices for these goods. China's productivity has improved fast enough to offset increases in rural wages and ensure its competitiveness at the labour-intensive end of the spectrum. At the higher-technology end export growth has been based on a combination of growing domestic capability and the activities of multinational companies (MNCs) in relocating segments of the production chain to China to take advantage of low labour costs. The key to the PRC's further progress here will lie in its own capability development[3].

The sheer speed, magnitude and range of China's export expansion have raised worries that competing countries are losing their overseas markets and FDI inflows. Latin America, as a more industrialised region than the PRC (its manufactured value added per capita in 2000 was nearly double that of the PRC, at $627 as compared with $350, UNIDO, 2004) is a potential competitor, particularly in the US market. The most direct threat has been perceived to be in Mexico (see Chapter 2 in this book).

The popular notion of "competitive threat" comes from business, where companies compete with one another and a gain in share by one is necessarily a loss by another. Transposing this to the national level means that trade is also a zero-sum game where one country gains at the expense of another. The loss of markets thus means a loss of jobs, incomes and growth. To the economist, this approach is misleading. The loss of markets in one industry does not imply that the country as a whole is less competitive. Countries trade with each other in a range of products and it is unclear what higher or lower competitiveness means for an economy as a whole. The United States, for instance, is becoming less competitive in making apparel and more competitive in making computers, but is it meaningful that the country as a whole is becoming "less" or "more" competitive?

Krugman (1994) argues that it is not. To him, "Competitiveness is a meaningless word when applied to national economies. And the obsession with competitiveness is both wrong and dangerous." (p. 44). "International trade is not a zero-sum game" and treating it as such shows a lack of understanding of basic trade theory (p. 34). If all parties gain from specialising in trade, the entry of a new competitor can raise welfare for all partners – there is no competitive threat".

Krugman uses the simple Heckscher-Ohlin (H-O) model to make his case. With efficient markets, perfect information, identical production functions across countries, no scale economies, no learning, full employment, fully mobile factors within economies, exogenous technical change and all the other assumptions of static H-O models, all participants benefit from trade. The rise or fall of particular activities is irrelevant and the opening of trade (or the entry of a new player) leads to a new equilibrium in which again all participants are better off. In this model, the pattern of specialisation does not matter. Because there are no externalities, innovation or differentiated products, all activities are equally beneficial and all factors yield equal returns at the margin. The size of the entrant and its rate of export growth also do not matter, because adjustment is instantaneous and costless.

Does this dispose of the "competitive threat"? Unfortunately, no. The result depends crucially on the assumptions of the canonical H-O model. If these assumptions are relaxed to allow for greater realism – scale economies, differentiated products, adjustment lags, uncertainty, technological gaps, externalities and agglomeration effects, endogenous technical change, cumulative learning, information failures, unemployment, immobile factors domestically and mobile ones abroad, large firms with market power and so on – the outcome can be quite different. Benefits remain from specialisation and trade remains a non-zero sum game, but the realisation of the benefits in imperfect markets depends on the ability of each economy to create (or attract) competitive capabilities and to move into activities that offer the best opportunities for growth, technological development and spillover benefits (here the structure of comparative advantage does matter).

Perspectives on international trade alternative to the simple H-O model help to clarify the adjustment problem. For example, the "new economic geography" (ironically also associated with Krugman, 1998) views trade through models where increasing returns to scale, learning and externalities have an important role. This alternative type of trade model predicts strong tendencies toward geographical concentration and clustering with cumulative gains. International dispersal of activities like manufacturing (but the arguments apply to any sector with increasing returns) requires either large cost increases in established production centres (due for example to rising wages or congestion costs) or major falls in trade costs.

Recent globalisation trends can be interpreted as a process of falling trade costs that include not just transport costs and import tariffs or tariff equivalents, but also the less obvious time costs of goods in transit, search costs as trading partners seek each other out, control and management costs in organising supply chains internationally and unofficial policy barriers, including unofficial payments. Falls in trade cost, in fact, have been shown empirically to have a relatively large impact on trade flows. In the 1990s, the PRC, with its large labour surplus and increasingly outward policy orientation and openness to FDI, was well placed to take advantage of these cost decreases.

The prediction of these models is that the de-concentration process will itself be highly inequitable, and a limited number of new, dispersed production centres will emerge (Puga and Venables, 1996). Hence economies that lack the flexibility to move quickly into increasing-return activities may find that once producers in rival economies become established the process of catch-up may be lengthy and difficult. From this perspective, the rise of the first and second tier Newly Industrialized Economies (NIEs), in part the result of FDI flows from the older established producer, Japan, represents one of stage industrial dispersal. Rapid growth in the PRC, a more recent dispersal stage, is also strongly influenced by FDI flows, in part from the NIEs themselves. The question at hand, therefore, is "What are the implications of this more recent dispersal of production for the economies of Latin America?"

The entry of a large, efficient low-wage competitor like China into new export markets can involve significant adjustment costs, and where full and rapid adjustment is not attained it can lead to welfare losses. The outcome depends on two factors:

— The similarity of export structures in the competing countries, with greater similarity calling for greater adjustments on the part of the established producers; and

— The speed, cost, nature and extent of adjustment in each country. These depend on the efficiency of existing markets and institutions (and access to foreign capabilities), which in turn depends on the efficiency of policy to overcome market and institutional failures where they exist[4].

Lall and Albaladejo (2004) examine the problems of economies in East Asia (EA) adjusting to competition from the PRC. LAC has two advantages over EA: greater economic distance from the PRC and more different export structures (with more inter-industry complementarities). While some industries in LAC face direct and intense competition from China – the most obvious examples are electronics in Mexico and apparel in Mexico and Central America – LAC should, in general, face lower adjustment costs and benefit more from bilateral trade with the PRC (see Chapter 2 in this book).

At the same time, no LAC economy comes near the mature EA NIEs (Singapore, the Republic of Korea and Taipei,China) in terms of industrial capabilities[5], although the larger economies have pockets of advanced capabilities, like automobiles, pharmaceuticals and aircraft in Brazil. In general, however, the opportunities for LAC "keeping ahead" of the PRC in terms of product complexity are narrower. Certainly, no LAC country has the possibility of relocating industrial activities in the PRC to take advantage of its lower costs. In direct competition, therefore, it is more likely that LAC companies will find it more difficult to keep ahead. Moreover, the intra-industry or vertical "sharing" of export activity happening in EA is much less feasible between LAC and the PRC. Not only does economic distance place a barrier, but also the two main industries in which such sharing occurs, automobiles and electronics, have limited potential for intra-industry LAC-PRC trade. The PRC is not a major auto exporter and products are too heavy (in terms of value-to-weight ratios) to make such long-distance interchange feasible[6]. In electronics, the PRC is a major player and products are light enough to permit transcontinental production sharing (many hi-tech components originate in the United States). The major electronics exporter in Latin America, Mexico, has been losing exports and jobs to the PRC, although there are in fact some signs of intra-industry trade, and the net longer-term trend is unclear.

LAC may face a more serious threat over the long term. The export specialisation of most LAC countries is heavily biased towards resource-based and primary products. It is not geared to dynamic categories in world trade and offers few technological or skill benefits. Chinese growth may well constrain their future ability to diversify into more dynamic, technology-intensive products and so downgrade their potential comparative advantage. While one cannot analyse this possibility with past trade data, one can gauge from past trends the direction in which the region is heading.

Measuring the Competitive Threat

There is no accepted methodology for quantifying a "competitive threat" with the types of data available. In the business literature, the common measure of competitive performance is relative market shares. One can start with this – in the simplest case, there is a competitive threat if the PRC gains export market share and another country loses. The intensity of the threat is given by the extent of the relative change. The analysis looks at competitiveness both in world markets and in the main market for LAC, the United States.

Such market-share data do not show how LAC and the PRC actually interact with each other at the product level, however. While it is not possible to infer direct causal relationships for the competitive impact of Chinese entry (only detailed fieldwork can show such relationships), it is possible to make some progress by examining combinations of market-share changes for the PRC and other countries. The technique used in Lall and Albaladejo (2004), distinguishes five outcomes (Table 3.1) and quantifies the exports that fall under each over time.

Table 3.1. **Matrix of Competitive Interactions between the PRC and Another Country in Export Markets**

Chinese Export Market Shares	
Rising	Falling
A. No threat	**C. Reverse threat**
Both the PRC and the other country have rising market shares, and the latter is gaining more than the PRC	No competitive threat from the PRC. The threat is the reverse, from the other country to the PRC.
B. Partial threat	
Both are gaining market share but the PRC is gaining faster than the other country	
D. Direct threat	**E. Mutual withdrawal: no threat**
The PRC gains market share and the other country loses. This may indicate a causal connection unless the other country was losing market share in the absence of Chinese entry.	Both parties lose shares in export markets to other competitors.

Source: Authors.

All the measures are only suggestive, because the data cannot, as they stand, prove that the PRC causes a change in the export performance of the other country. Moreover each indicator has caveats. For instance, the data may suggest a "partial threat" when the PRC is raising market share faster than the other country (i.e. absent the PRC and given that the other country is competitive, its share may have risen faster). Yet it is possible that China helps the other country to compete better by complementing it within an integrated production network and so preventing its market share from doing even less well. This may be plausible for EA economies in some sectors but is much less so for LAC economies. In the "direct threat" the PRC gains and the other country loses market share. Within EA, this may be compatible with the losing country placing export facilities in China and so extending its competitive advantage (this happens with textiles and clothing and some electronics). For the PRC-LAC interaction this pattern is highly unlikely, so that a "direct threat" is unambiguously negative, and the share of the direct-threat category in an economy's total exports becomes the preferred measure of threat.

The potential for competition between LAC and the PRC is examined by measuring the similarity of their export structures over time at two levels:

1) At the broad technological level, the overlap between the PRC and LAC in primary products and four technological categories of manufactured exports: RB (resource based), LT (low technology), MT (medium technology) and HT (high technology) (see Table 3.2). These four categories are disaggregated into nine sub-categories, capturing different technological or structural features for further analysis. This technology classification offers several other benefits. It allows gauging the basis of each country's comparative advantage and its evolution over time. It shows how the country is positioned to benefit from innovation and from changes in global trade patterns, and it provides an indicator of whether the country will move up or down the technology ladder as a result of competitive interaction with the PRC[7]; and

Table 3.2. **Technological Classification of Exports**

Examples
Fresh fruit, meat, rice, cocoa, tea, coffee, wood, coal, crude petroleum, gas
Manufactured products
Prepared meats/fruits, beverages, wood products, vegetable oils
Ore concentrates, petroleum/rubber products, cement, cut gems, glass
Textile fabrics, clothing, headgear, footwear, leather manufactures, travel goods
Pottery, simple metal parts/structures, furniture, jewellery, toys, plastic products
Passenger vehicles and parts, commercial vehicles, motorcycles and parts
Synthetic fibres, chemicals and paints, fertilisers, plastics, iron, pipes/tubes
Engines, motors, industrial machinery, pumps, switchgear, ships, watches
Office/data processing/telecommunications equipment, TVs, transistors, turbines, power-generating equipment
Pharmaceuticals, aerospace, optical/measuring instruments, cameras
Electricity, cinema film, printed matter, "special" transactions, gold, art, coins, pets

Source: Lall (2000).

2) At the more detailed product level, the statistical correlation between the export structures of the PRC and LAC. Higher correlation indicates greater potential for direct competition and rising correlations over time show that this potential is growing.

To consider variations in competitive performance within Latin America, the analysis covers data for 1990-2002 for 18 countries with substantial industrial sectors. The countries are divided into the following groups:

- LAC: All the 18 countries below taken together;
- LAC-M: LAC excluding Mexico because Mexico becomes an outlier after 1995 when it joins NAFTA;
- LAC Big 3: Argentina, Brazil and Mexico;
- LAC Big 2: Argentina and Brazil only, again to exclude the outlier Mexico;
- LAC Medium 4: Chile, Colombia, Peru and Venezuela;
- LAC Small 11: Bolivia, Costa Rica, Ecuador, El Salvador, Guatemala, Honduras, Jamaica, Nicaragua, Panama, Paraguay and Uruguay.
- LAC S 10: The Small 11 excluding Costa Rica because its Intel plant dating from the late 1990s and resulting high-technology exports make it an outlier in the group.

Changes in World Market Shares

As a rough guide to trends in competitiveness, Table 3.3 considers changes in world market share (WMS) for LAC and the PRC, 1990-2002. The PRC gains WMS in all products, marginally in primary products and massively in LT and HT goods. For all exports LAC raised its world market share by two percentage points in the 1990s after losses in the 1980s. Its performance is very modest compared to the PRC and EA more generally, however, and in part it represents a catch-up from the losses of the previous decade. Surprisingly for a relatively resource-rich region, LAC's WMS in primary products barely changes (from 12.4 per cent in 1990 to 12.7 per cent in 2002. In manufactures, its WMS rises from 2.3 per cent to 4.9 per cent, with the main gains in complex MT and HT products (3.4 and 3 points respectively), but this improvement in the technological structure of LAC exports is due almost entirely to Mexico. Mexico accounts for almost all of LAC's improved WMS in pure manufactures (LT, MT and HT); the rest of the region (LAC-M) loses in LT while its gains in MT and HT are marginal (0.2 per cent and 0.4 per cent). In the resource-based

Table 3.3. **World Market Shares of Exports by the PRC, East Asia and LAC**
(per cent)

	EA 8 1990	EA 8 2002	PRC 1990	PRC 2002	LAC 18 1990	LAC 18 2002	LAC-M 1990	LAC-M 2002	Mexico 1990	Mexico 2002
All products	9.99	11.09	2.03	5.96	3.86	5.89	2.98	2.95	0.87	2.95
Primary Products	8.15	5.85	2.72	2.86	12.38	12.72	9.62	9.98	2.76	2.74
Manufactured	10.33	11.87	1.90	6.42	2.28	4.87	1.76	1.90	0.52	2.98
Resource based	8.62	8.32	1.35	3.23	4.74	5.85	4.18	4.80	0.56	1.05
Agro-based	9.22	7.33	1.43	2.89	5.74	8.59	5.23	7.01	0.51	1.58
Mineral-based	8.35	8.72	1.31	3.36	4.29	4.73	3.70	3.90	0.58	0.84
Low technology	17.69	11.57	4.97	14.85	2.29	4.75	1.92	1.78	0.37	2.98
Fashion cluster	24.46	14.23	8.07	21.13	2.71	5.06	2.47	2.15	0.25	2.91
Other LT	12.11	9.61	2.41	10.21	1.95	4.52	1.47	1.50	0.48	3.02
Medium technology	6.44	8.25	1.27	3.84	1.78	5.20	1.09	1.33	0.69	3.87
Automotive	1.82	3.83	1.12	0.88	2.16	6.01	0.84	1.26	1.32	4.75
Process	8.02	10.86	1.36	3.72	3.09	4.18	2.39	2.77	0.70	1.41
Engineering	8.74	10.35	1.33	6.09	0.90	5.06	0.64	0.73	0.27	4.33
High technology	13.60	21.11	0.56	6.98	0.61	3.66	0.38	0.76	0.23	2.90
Electronics	20.18	31.45	0.45	9.78	0.47	4.18	0.20	0.49	0.27	3.69
Other HT	3.11	3.69	0.74	2.27	0.84	2.78	0.67	1.21	0.17	1.57

	LAC big 2 1990	LAC big 2 2002	LAC med 4 1990	LAC med 4 2002	LAC small 11 1990	LAC small 11 2002	LAC small 10 1990	LAC small 10 2002
All products	1.44	1.55	1.20	1.06	0.38	0.39	0.34	0.30
Primary Products	2.84	3.90	5.78	5.23	1.57	1.39	1.39	1.21
Manufactured	1.19	1.20	0.36	0.44	0.16	0.24	0.14	0.17
Resource based	2.56	2.71	0.98	1.38	0.48	0.62	0.45	0.55
Agro-based	3.69	4.28	0.87	1.63	0.60	1.28	0.55	1.09
Mineral-based	2.05	2.07	1.03	1.27	0.43	0.36	0.41	0.32
Low technology	1.20	1.03	0.46	0.42	0.22	0.32	0.18	0.22
Fashion cluster	1.48	1.31	0.61	0.48	0.37	0.39	0.33	0.26
Other LT	0.97	0.83	0.33	0.38	0.10	0.26	0.06	0.19
Medium technology	0.88	0.97	0.15	0.25	0.04	0.10	0.03	0.06
Automotive	0.80	1.12	0.03	0.13	0.01	0.02	0.01	0.02
Process	1.73	1.68	0.48	0.79	0.13	0.20	0.11	0.17
Engineering	0.53	0.52	0.07	0.09	0.02	0.12	0.01	0.03
High technology	0.32	0.57	0.02	0.05	0.03	0.13	0.02	0.02
Electronics	0.19	0.32	0.01	0.02	0.00	0.15	0.00	0.00
Other HT	0.54	1.00	0.04	0.11	0.07	0.11	0.05	0.06

Note: The EA 8 are Singapore, Korea, Chinese Taipei, PRC, Indonesia, Malaysia, Philippines, Thailand.
Source: UN Comtrade database.

categories, Mexico loses in primary products and gains slightly in RB manufactures, while LAC-M gains small market shares in both. In all pure manufactured export categories Mexico is a larger exporter than the rest of LAC put together. In absolute terms, LAC-M remains a tiny global player (with under 2 per cent WMS) in all segments apart from primary and RB products, fashion products and process industries.

Within LAC, Argentina and Brazil (LAC-Big 2) perform very poorly. Their manufactured WMS stagnates at just over 1 per cent, but these two economies show different industrial trends – rises in WMS of 0.2 points or more in primary products, agro-based RB, automotives and other HT (aircraft and pharmaceuticals), offset by declines in LT and process MT products. The Med 4 (Chile, Colombia, Peru and Venezuela) suffer a loss in primary products with gains in RB, automotives, MT process and other HT. The 11 small LAC economies lose in primary products and gain in agro-based RB, other LT, process and engineering MT, and electronics. Within this group all the gain in electronics comes from Costa Rica. Several small LAC economies depend heavily on fashion-cluster exports, but their WMS declines once Costa Rica is excluded.

In summary, LAC without Mexico does poorly, raising its world market share in all manufactured exports by less than 0.2 percentage points; the two large economies, Argentina and Brazil, have the weakest performance. The largest world market shares held by LAC-M are in primary and resource-based products and MT process industries, all of which offer relatively low technological and other spillover benefits and tend to grow slowly in trade. Mexico, by contrast, behaves like an EA NIE, with significant gains across the spectrum (primary products excepted). Similarly, for a group of the "50 most dynamic products in world trade", Latin America's (LAC-18) share in exports at 46 per cent in 2002 broadly matches both that of the PRC (48 per cent) and that in world trade as a whole (50 per cent). The inclusion of Mexico strongly biases this comparison, however, and excluding it drops the LAC-M share of these dynamic products to 36 per cent[8].

Potential for Competition

This section considers LAC's "potential for competition" with PRC in terms of exports to third markets, starting with the similarity of structures; the hypothesis is simply that the greater the similarity in export structures, the greater the potential threat from the PRC – given its lower wages and faster expansion. Table 3.4 shows the distribution of regional exports by technology.

Table 3.4. **Technology Structure of Regional Exports**
(Per cent)

	World 1990	World 2002	PRC 1990	PRC 2002	LAC 18 1990	LAC 18 2002	LAC-M 1990	LAC-M 2002	LAC Big 2 1990	LAC Big 2 2002
Primary Products	15.6	13.0	21.0	6.2	50.1	28.0	50.3	44.0	30.7	32.7
Resource based	17.0	15.6	11.3	8.4	20.9	15.5	23.8	25.4	30.2	27.2
Agro-based	5.3	4.5	3.8	2.2	7.9	6.6	9.3	10.7	13.6	12.4
Mineral-based	11.7	11.1	7.5	6.3	13.0	8.9	14.5	14.7	16.6	14.8
Low technology	16.7	15.4	41.0	38.5	10.0	12.4	10.8	9.3	13.9	10.3
Fashion cluster	7.6	6.6	30.1	23.3	5.3	5.6	6.3	4.8	7.8	5.6
Other LT	9.2	8.9	10.9	15.2	4.6	6.8	4.5	4.5	6.1	4.7
Medium technology	36.3	35.6	22.8	22.9	16.8	31.4	13.3	16.1	22.1	22.2
Automotive	11.2	12.0	6.2	1.8	6.3	12.3	3.2	5.2	6.2	8.7
Process	8.1	7.4	5.4	4.6	6.5	5.2	6.5	6.%	9.7	8.0
Engineering	17.0	16.2	11.1	16.6	4.0	13.9	3.6	4.0	6.2	5.5
High technology	14.4	20.4	4.0	23.9	2.3	12.7	1.8	5.2	3.2	7.6
Electronics	8.8	12.8	1.9	21.0	1.1	9.1	0.6	2.1	1.2	2.7
Other HT	5.5	7.6	2.0	2.9	1.2	3.6	1.2	3.1	2.1	4.9

	LAC Med 4 1990	LAC Med 4 2002	LAC Small 11 1990	LAC Small 11 2002	LAC Small 10 1990	LAC Small 10 2002	Mexico 1990	Mexico 2002
Primary Products	75.0	64.2	64.1	46.3	64.1	52.2	49.4	12.1
Resource based	13.8	20.3	21.3	24.8	22.6	28.3	10.9	5.6
Agro-based	3.8	6.9	8.4	14.7	8.6	16.4	3.1	2.4
Mineral-based	10.0	13.4	12.9	10.1	14.0	11.9	7.8	3.2
Low technology	6.4	6.2	9.6	12.6	9.1	11.3	7.2	15.6
Fashion cluster	3.8	3.0	7.3	6.6	7.3	5.8	2.1	6.5
Other LT	2.5	3.2	2.4	6.0	1.7	5.5	5.0	9.1
Medium technology	4.6	8.3	3.8	9.4	3.4	6.5	28.7	46.7
Automotive	0.3	1.4	0.2	0.7	0.2	0.8	17.1	19.4
Process	3.2	5.5	2.7	3.8	2.5	4.0	6.4	3.5
Engineering	1.0	1.4	1.0	4.8	0.6	1.6	5.2	23.8
High technology	0.3	1.0	1.1	6.9	0.9	1.6	3.8	20.1
Electronics	0.1	0.2	0.0	4.8	0.1	0.1	2.7	16.1
Other HT	0.2	0.8	1.1	2.1	0.9	1.5	1.1	4.0

Source: UN Comtrade data base.

Technological Structure of Exports

LAC has a much more limited focus than EA does on technologically sophisticated goods with dynamic market prospects[9]. Within LAC, Mexico (like the PRC) shows a sharp decline in the share of primary and RB products over the period covered here. Mexico also behaves similarly to the PRC in terms of the growing share of HT, but has a much lower share for LT products, counter-balanced by a higher MT share. The Big 2, Medium 4 and Small 11 LAC economies all have high shares of primary and RB exports, with the larger economies having proportionately more MT exports. At the more disaggregated technology level, the highest reliance on mineral-based RB exports is in the Medium 4 (the impact of oil in Venezuela). Fashion-cluster exports are relatively important for the Small 11, due to US outsourcing of apparel in the Caribbean and Central America (this came under severe competitive threat from the PRC when the Multi Fibre Agreement expired at the end of 2004). MT process industries are significant for the Big 2 and the Medium 4, while auto products are most significant for Mexico and the Big 2. MT engineering exports are very significant in Mexico but not in other LAC economies; electronics are also large in Mexico and (because of Costa Rica) in the Small 11. Other HT exports are significant only in the Big 2. Mexico apart, the PRC has a technological trade pattern very different from that in LAC. These technology comparisons are fairly aggregate, but they do suggest that Chinese exports do not pose a direct threat to the bulk of LAC exports, with some exceptions:

- Fashion products (of interest to the smaller economies and Mexico);

- "Other LT" (This is a broad category, but the PRC may pose a threat in specific products like toys, sports goods or travel goods that the smaller economies export.);

- Engineering products, where PRC is now a major exporter of machinery and consumer durables and may affect similar exports from Mexico and possibly Brazil. Their relative weight raises transport costs, however, and this may reduce their competitiveness in markets to which LAC countries sell; and

- Electronics, of export interest mainly to Mexico and Costa Rica.

Product Structure

The export structures of LAC and the PRC can be compared by product category (examined here at the three-digit level for 181 products, excluding "special transactions") without categorising them by technology. One can start with the stability of export structures in each country, as shown by the correlation between export patterns in 1990 and 2002. A high coefficient shows that the export composition is relatively unchanging, while a low coefficient indicates structural change. The more changeable structures are in the PRC and Mexico (with correlation coefficients of roughly 0.4 and 0.6 respectively), and the least are the LAC Medium 4 and LAC without Mexico (correlation coefficients of over 0.9). More rapid structural change – if it allows the exporter to respond to shifting structures in world trade – should lead to faster growth. The data bear this out; a regression of the stability coefficients on export growth rates over 1990-2002 for the sample countries in LAC and PRC supports the expectation. The adjusted R-square is 0.31 (F = 11.2), and the coefficient is negative and significant at – 0.022 (t = –3.35). The high degree of export-structure stability in LAC, along with a specialisation in non-dynamic products, appears to be taking a toll in the growth of export earnings.

In a comparison of the export structures of individual LAC countries with that of the PRC, for all products Chinese exports overlap significantly only with Mexico and Costa Rica, and even here the correlation coefficients are relatively low, at only 0.47 and 0.27 respectively. Thereafter the coefficients drop sharply; all other LAC countries have almost no correlation with Chinese exports. In contrast, the PRC's export structure and that of the main EA producers has a correlation coefficient of 0.75 for 2002 (Lall and Albaladejo, 2004).

Taking manufactured products only, a fairly dramatic decline occurs over time in the similarity of Chinese exports with most LAC exports, due to the rapid structural shifts in the former. Only Mexico and Costa Rica have any significant similarity to the PRC in 2002, with correlation coefficients of around 0.5 and 0.35 respectively. Most other countries have correlations with PRC that are either negative or below 0.1. Even excluding RB products (where the PRC is least specialised) raises the correlation only slightly. In terms of the current overlap, therefore, the PRC seems to pose a very small threat to the bulk of LAC exports, including the large industrial producers of Argentina and Brazil; even excluding RB products their coefficients for 2002 are -0.1 and 0.13 respectively.

Competitive Impact on LAC in World Markets

Turn now to the fivefold matrix of competitive effects of the PRC on LAC, starting with the world market, then considering the US market alone (see Table 3.1 for definitions of the threat categories). At the three-digit SITC level and for 1990-2002, changes in WMS have been calculated based on a comparison of growth rates for LAC countries and the PRC. For the two years 1990 and 2002 one thus can show the proportions of trade taken by the five threat categories. As noted earlier, these calculations can only be suggestive – they cannot prove causation – but nonetheless they are plausible and interesting. Table 3.5 summarises the position for Latin America as a whole (LAC-18) in the world market. Lall *et al.* (2005) gives more detailed data for each country as well as for the five main products that fall under each category.

Table 3.5. **The PRC Competitive Threat in World Markets for The LAC 18**

	Values ($ million) 1990	Values ($ million) 2002	Distribution (Per cent) 1990	Distribution (Per cent) 2002
Partial Threat	17 164.8	91 288.9	14.6	28.0
No Threat	12 661.4	102 644.9	10.8	31.5
Direct Threat	35 809.9	3 142.1	30.5	11.4
PRC under Threat	14 229.0	4 648.8	12.1	14.6
Mutual Withdrawal	37 538.4	47 253.8	32.0	14.5
Total	117 03.4	325 978.5	100.0	100.0

Source: UN Comtrade data base.

Large variations by country appear in the competitive threat from the PRC, and the nature of the threat changes significantly for several countries. For the world market and for all the LAC 18 countries together, the average weighted share of threatened exports – those under direct plus partial threat – is surprisingly stable at 45.1 per cent in 1990 and 39.4 per cent in 2002 (Table 3.5). A shift also occurs in the composition of the threat, from direct to partial, so its intensity decreases significantly over time (this is also true of EA, although there the degree of threat is much higher, with 75 per cent of exports (on an unweighted basis) under some form of threat (Lall and Albaladejo, 2004)[10]. Eleven per cent of LAC exports fell into the direct-threat category in 2002.

At the country level and in terms of both direct and partial threat in 1990 and 2002, the least threatened country is Venezuela (with less than 20 per cent of exports in these two categories), shielded by its heavy dependence on oil-based exports. The countries with the largest reduction in the competitive threat in these two categories are Paraguay, Peru and Argentina; all have moved over time into primary or RB products, where the PRC does not have a strong competitive position, or into products like automobiles, where the PRC is not yet a significant exporter. Countries like Guatemala and Colombia appear to place the PRC under threat, because they gain market share in primary products, where it is a small exporter and is losing market share.

The most threatened countries in LAC in total exports are Costa Rica, El Salvador and Chile (over 70 per cent of total exports are under threat for the first two and around 60 per cent for Chile). While the presence of Chile as a highly threatened country may appear surprising, it reflects the large share of its exports in copper, where China gains WMS while Chile loses. Its large exports of fish appear partially threatened because here too the PRC gains more WMS than it does. In Costa Rica the Chinese threat is overwhelmingly partial, with the PRC gaining WMS in electronics, instruments, apparel and processed food exports. El Salvador faces direct and partial threat in the textile and clothing industry. In the more serious direct-threat category, all countries see a decline in its share of their exports in 1990-2002, and seven (Costa Rica, Ecuador, El Salvador, Guatemala, Mexico, Panama and Venezuela) have less than 10 per cent of their exports in this category. The most directly threatened are now Chile, Bolivia, Brazil, Uruguay and Colombia, all with more than 20 per cent of their exports here.

While earlier export-structure comparisons show that Mexico faces the greatest potential threat from China, this calculation shows that because of its very rapid gains in WMS it did not actually face a significant threat over 1990-2002. The directly threatened exports, in which Mexico loses WMS and the PRC gains, constituted only 1.6 per cent of its exports in 2002, down from nearly 10 per cent in 1990. The "partially threatened" exports are much larger, 32 per cent in 2002, up from 19 per cent in 1990, and they comprise mainly electronic and electrical products and furniture. These may turn into direct threats if, post-2002 when this data analysis stops, the PRC continues to gain market share and actually takes markets away from Mexico. Brazil faces a larger competitive threat (28 per cent direct and 23 per cent partial in 2002), but the extent of the direct threat declines substantially, from 46 per cent in 1990. The largest partially threatened exports for Brazil are telecoms and footwear. On the other hand, its largest single export, aircraft, faces no threat from the PRC.

The next test looks at the types of products in which Latin America countries are losing market share most rapidly, using a simple correlation analysis. At the three-digit SITC level it correlates relative changes in market share in 1990-2002 (the growth of PRC exports minus the growth of Latin American exports) with first the growth of world exports for the product concerned and second the degree of specialisation of Latin American exporters (as measured by the revealed comparative advantage ratio, RCA). This correlation analysis is done for LAC as a group and for individual countries. For all countries, the loss of market share to the PRC is greatest in the fastest-growing categories. For LAC as a group the correlation coefficient, although relatively low (0.16), is significant at the 1 per cent level. For Mexico it is higher (0.32) and again strongly significant. As far as the degree of specialisation is concerned, there is some evidence that LAC has held its position better in its more specialised product lines. The correlation coefficient between RCA in 2002 and relative export growth is negative and significant at the 1 per cent level for LAC as a group (-0.19) and for Mexico (-0.24), but not for many other individual countries. It also does not hold for specialisation (RCA) at the beginning of the period, 1990.

These results suggest that while potential for a competitive threat exists, LAC faces a significantly smaller threat overall than does EA, for two reasons. First, export structures as compared with the PRC differ far more, and, second, the structural similarities that do exist have yet to translate into a genuine market-share challenge. The evidence for this is that if for 2002 one ranks LAC countries by the correlation coefficient of their total export structures with that of PRC and compares this ranking with a ranking of the degree of direct threat (the direct threat category as a share of total exports) there is a significant negative correlation. The Spearman rank correlation coefficient is −0.504 (significant at the 1 per cent level). In other words, the countries with the more similar export structures show lower degrees of export threat. The clearest example is Mexico, the LAC country with the greatest similarity, which grew sufficiently rapidly over the 1990s to avoid a loss of WMS to the PRC. It remains to be seen whether this will continue.

Table 3.6 illustrates a similar competitive-impact exercise for the US market[11]. The PRC accounted for 12 per cent of US imports in 2002 compared with just 3 per cent in 1990. Its gain of over eight percentage points was nearly double of that of the LAC 18 (note that LAC-M lost US market share, almost entirely in RB products). Latin America as a whole (LAC-18) had a share of 17 per cent in 2002, but 11 per cent of this of this is due to Mexico alone. China accounts for about twice as much of US imports of LT products as the LAC 18 and for almost as much of HT imports. By 2002, it overtook Mexico in HT products (it lagged in 2000) and almost matched it in RB products.

Table 3.6. **Competitive Threat from the PRC in the US Market for the LAC 18**

	Values ($ million)		Distribution (Per cent)	
	1990	2002	1990	2002
Partial Threat	3 913.2	20 777.3	8.5	10.8
No Threat	7 508.3	101 371.3	16.3	52.7
Direct Threat	13 663.2	14 567.0	29.6	7.6
PRC under Threat	10 740.6	42 442.7	23.3	22.1
Mutual Withdrawal	10 267.9	13 238.9	22.3	6.9
Total	46 093.2	192 397.2	100.0	100.0

Source: UN Comtrade Database.

In comparison with the analysis of the world market there are similarities as well as differences. In terms of total threat (direct plus partial) Venezuela continues in both exercises as the least threatened country in LAC. In 2002, Paraguay appears as the most threatened country in the US market. Costa Rica had this position in the world market as a whole, but now appears in about the middle of the threat ranks for the US market. Mexico seems even less threatened than in world markets, while Brazil looks somewhat more threatened. Argentina also moves up in the threat ranks.

By the preferred indicator of direct threat, all LAC appears to have a smaller share of its US export market directly threatened in 2002 than in 1990. The most threatened countries are now Chile (around 40 per cent of its trade), followed by Argentina and Uruguay with around 35 per cent and Brazil with 30 per cent. The main products involved are copper (Chile), fruits (Chile, Brazil), petroleum products (Argentina, Brazil), sugar and fish (Uruguay) and internal combustion engines (Brazil), none of which are goods in which the PRC might be expected to have an obvious comparative advantage over LAC. The least threatened countries are Costa Rica, Mexico, Panama and Venezuela, all with less than 10 per cent of their trade with the United States in this category. In 2002 a serious threat to Mexico in particular does not show up. By this measure only about 3 per cent of its exports to the United States are directly threatened. In a correlation analysis similar to that for the world market there is a tendency for the growth of China's exports relative to that of individual LAC countries to be higher in the faster-growing categories of US imports, but this result is significant neither for LAC as a group nor for Mexico. For LAC-M there is a weak correlation of 0.15 (significant at the 5 per cent level).

In terms of bilateral trade, LAC currently runs a large and growing deficit with the PRC; PRC accounted for just under 5 per cent of total LAC imports in 2003. Moving from a surplus of $175 million in 1980, LAC as whole ran a deficit with PRC of $5.5 billion in 2002. Not every country is in deficit; in 2002 five of the LAC 18 ran surpluses with the PRC, including Argentina and Brazil. The largest deficit, for Mexico, exceeded that of the LAC 18. The deficits are all in non-resource based products. In 2002, primary products and RB manufactures showed surpluses of $2.3 billion and $1 billion respectively. These are offset by much larger deficits in manufactures: LT products ($3 billion), MT products ($2.8 billion) and HT products ($3 billion). This illustrates clearly the structural shift in the pattern of competitiveness in LAC towards resource-based products and away from both simple low-technology manufactures and more complex medium and high technology products.

Hence a new pattern of specialisation is emerging in LAC-PRC bilateral trade, with LAC as a net exporter of primary and resource-based products and a net importer of manufactures. Some countries in LAC benefit from growing PRC imports of primary and RB products. Yet because this bilateral trade accounts for only tiny shares of their total trade one cannot assume that it can have significant effects on their overall patterns. LAC accounted for only 2.4 per cent of Chinese exports and the PRC for less than 2 per cent of LAC's exports in 2002. The main competitive arena is thus the United States (which took over 20 per cent of the PRC's exports in 2002 and nearly 60 per cent of LAC's), with the EU some distance behind. The real effects of the Chinese threat are likely to be felt here, although little direct evidence has yet emerged of this threat being very substantial.

Conclusions

The idea of an economy facing a competitive threat has been much discussed. In a world of instant adjustment, trade diversion as an economy's market share is taken by a lower-cost or higher-quality competitor will pose no problems. In practice and once a whole range of real-world considerations is introduced, growth can be cumulative and export success in dynamic products with strong learning externalities can place an economy on a higher growth path than a concentration on an alternative set of simpler export goods. The current trading environment is characterised not just by a lowering of tariff barriers through the WTO, but also by major reductions in transport and communications costs leading to a fall in trade cost more broadly. In this situation the rise of the PRC is important both because its size and rapid growth suggest important trade creation effects as it provides an expanding market for others and because it is becomingly increasingly competitive in a wide range of goods in both low and high technology categories.

Latin America remains somewhat distant from this process. Some countries benefit from growing Chinese imports of primary and RB products, although in general the PRC remains a relatively small market for LAC, notwithstanding that it overtook Japan as an import supplier to the region in 2003. The trade structure of most of LAC is generally more complementary than competitive with that of the PRC. With a differing export structure the likelihood of damaging trade-diversion effects weakens. The exceptions, principally Mexico and Costa Rica, are closely integrated into production networks of MNCs similarly to the PRC.

The analysis here has provided a simple framework for classifying trade data on the basis of "competitive threats". In general LAC's threatened trade (directly plus partially), at just below 40 per cent of all trade, lies well below the comparable figure for EA. Goods in the more serious direct-threat category make up only 10 per cent of total trade. The two LAC economies with export structures most similar to China's, Mexico and Costa Rica, have very low shares of trade in the direct-threat category (2 per cent and 6 per cent, respectively) although their shares in the partial-threat groups are far higher (32 per cent and 69 per cent respectively). Considering the US market alone, the direct-threat groups remain small and the partial-threat share is also much lower (8 per cent for Mexico and 33 per cent for Costa Rica), reflecting rapid export growth to the United States from these economies up to 2002.

These basic results on competitive threats have some caveats. Apart from the problems of attributing causation, the past may not be a good guide to the future, particularly as far as the rather sanguine result for Mexico goes. Ironically, the long-time suspicion of export-oriented FDI in Latin America may prove relevant here, if in the face of falling trade costs that lower the disadvantage of distant production locations MNCs decide to shift from bases in Mexico and Central America to take advantage of lower labour costs in the PRC. This process, at least as much as competition from PRC exports, produces the real challenge to policy makers in serving the US market.

The analysis of bilateral trade between LAC and the PRC reveals a striking tendency towards a pattern of specialisation with LAC a net exporter of primary products and a net importer of manufactures. The patterns of the two regions present almost a classic textbook illustration of trade between developing and industrialised regions, where the former (LAC) strengthens its specialisation in primary products and processes resources while the latter (the PRC) does the reverse. The surprise is that LAC is the richer region, with a longer history of modern industrialisation, more human resources, more FDI per capita and more liberal trade and investment regimes. The result is arguably a downgrading of comparative advantage in a dynamic sense, surprising for such a relatively industrialised region.

The non-threatened LAC countries – which have such different specialisations that they do not face Chinese competition in the United States or elsewhere – may nonetheless face a serious threat to their long-term development. A heavy reliance on primary and resource-based products is not conducive to dynamic comparative advantage or to technological upgrading, yet any such upgrading may well face a strong competitive threat from the PRC because it will already have "taken" the kinds of products they may feasibly move into. The issue then becomes much less about current competition and more about the future spaces open for the development of industrial exports in a liberalised world in which the PRC is pre-empting many markets for products that developing countries can export. LAC will remain a high-wage location relative to the PRC for the foreseeable future, and it will have to invest in higher levels of skill or technological competence to offset this. As yet there is little sign that it is doing so (see Lall, Albaladejo and Moreira, 2004).

Notes

1. The late Sanjaya Lall was Professor of Development Economics, University of Oxford, at the International Development Centre, Queen Elizabeth House. John Weiss is Professor of Economics at the University of Bradford and was previously Director of Research at the Asian Development Bank Institute at Tokyo. This research was supported by the Asian Development Bank Institute, Tokyo. Earlier versions of this paper are in ADB Institute Research Paper number 65, 2006 and in Oxford Development Studies, vol 33, no 2, June, 2005.

2. All the trade data in this paper are in current US dollars and come from the UN Comtrade database.

3. For a discussion of the role of capabilities (defined simply in terms of a combination of cost and quality) in trade and of the process of capability development see Sutton (2000). By one simple measure of its development, R&D expenditure per capita, the PRC has made great strides in recent years. In R&D, according to the 2004 OECD *Science, Technology and Innovation Scoreboard*, PRC reached 1.1 per cent of GDP in 2002, up from 0.6 per cent in 1996; around 60 per cent of the R&D expenditure came from companies rather than the government. In terms of business enterprise R&D as a share of GDP, this takes PRC to fourth place in the developing world, after the Republic of Korea, Taipei, China and Singapore well ahead of other large economies like India, Brazil, Mexico, Argentina or Indonesia.

4. Countries may also suffer because Chinese imports raise world prices for primary and intermediate products. This paper ignores this and other price effects, as it does not deal with unit price data (these are only available for a small set of traded products). The risk of PRC raising primary product prices is very real, however, and it attracts considerable media attention.

5. See Lall, Albaladejo and Moreira (2004).

6. See Lall, Albaladejo and Zhang (2004).

7. The technology classification is explained in detail in Lall (2000) and has been used in a number of recent studies on trade.

8. These are the 50 fastest-growing products on the world market at the three-digit SITC Rev 2 level for exports over $10 billion in 2000 (*i.e.* excluding small exports that grow rapidly from a low base).

9. See also Weiss and Jalilian (2004).

10. The unweighted average for threatened exports in EA of 75 per cent is much higher than LAC's unweighted average of 47 per cent. The highest figures for LAC are 75 per cent for Costa Rica and 71 per cent for El Salvador, while in EA they are 98 per cent for Hong Kong, China and 85 per cent for Malaysia. The lowest figure in LAC is 16 per cent for Venezuela, while in EA it is 50 per cent for Indonesia.

11. The competitive impact calculations below are carried out on the basis of export figures for each country to the United States (with market shares based on world exports to the USA) rather than on US import figures. The export figures are used to make the results comparable with the previous world market exercise. A calculation with US import data may well yield slightly different results.

Bibliography

KRUGMAN, P. (1994), "Competitiveness: A Dangerous Obsession", *Foreign Affairs*, Vol. 73, No. 2, 28-44.

KRUGMAN, P. (1998), "What's New About Economic Geography?", *Oxford Review of Economic Policy*, Vol. 14, No. 2, 7-17.

LALL, S. (2000), "The Technological Structure and Performance of Developing Country Manufactured Exports, 1985-98", *Oxford Development Studies*, Vol. 28, No. 3, 337-69.

LALL, S AND J. WEISS, WITH THE ASSISTANCE OF H. OIKAWA (2005), "China's Competitive Threat to Latin America: An Analysis for 1990-2002", *Oxford Development Studies*, Vol. 33, No. 2.

LALL, S. AND M. ALBALADEJO (2004), "China's Competitive Performance: A Threat to East Asian Manufactured Exports?", *World Development*, Vol. 32, No. 9, September.

LALL, S., M. ALBALADEJO AND M.M. MOREIRA (2004), *Latin American Industrial Competitiveness and the Challenge of Globalization*, Inter-American Development Bank, Integration and Regional Programs Department, INTAL-ITD Occasional Paper-SITI-05, Washington, D.C..

LALL, S., M. ALBALADEJO AND J. ZHANG (2004), "Mapping Fragmentation: Electronics and Automobiles in East Asia and Latin America", *Oxford Development Studies*, Vol. 32, No. 3, 407-432.

PUGA, D AND A. VENABLES (1996), "The Spread of Industry: Spatial Agglomeration and Economic Development" *Journal of Japanese International Economics*, Vol. 10, No. 4, 440-464.

SUTTON, J. (2000), "Rich Trades and Scarce Capabilities", Keynes Lecture, British Academy, mimeo.

UNIDO (2004), *Industrial Development Report 2004*, United Nations Industrial Development Organization, Vienna.

WEISS, J. AND H. JALILIAN (2004) "Industrialization in an Age of Globalization: Some Comparisons between East and South East Asia and Latin America", *Oxford Development Studies*, Vol. 32, No. 2, 283-308.

Chapter 4

Competing with the Dragon: Latin American and Chinese Exports to the US Market

by Ernesto López-Córdova, Alejandro Micco and Danielken Molina[1]

> **Abstract**
>
> How sensitive are Latin American exports to the impact of Chinese competition in the United States, their main market? This chapter calculates US import-substitution elasticities and uses them to estimate changes in Latin American and Chinese market shares under three scenarios: a substantial appreciation of the Chinese currency, regional free trade in the Americas and full elimination of US import quotas on textiles and apparel. The first two of these international policy shifts would benefit Latin American exports in US markets, and the third would not, but all three effects are not as large as one might imagine. External events cannot suffice to redress Latin America's relatively poor trade performance *vis-à-vis* China. The authors suggest attention throughout the region to policies that could boost its productivity performance.

Introduction

The recent emergence of China on the international economic scene is a momentous event profoundly transforming the world. Not a day goes by without headlines announcing how the Asian giant impacts commodity prices, capital flows, current account balances and factor and goods markets around the globe. Reactions to the way China affects the world economy vary from hope to fear to outright fatalism. Some observers see China as a vast and brisk market with enormous growth potential and opportunities. Others see it as a disruptive threat to existing industries in higher-wage countries. Still others feel there is little countries can do to cope with the mixture of threats and opportunities that China represents.

This wide range of views can be found in Latin America and the Caribbean (LAC). Whereas, for example, Southern Cone countries have benefited from the increased demand and consequent price rises of copper, iron ore, soybeans and other primary products, Central American and Caribbean countries have felt the brunt of Chinese export competition in world apparel markets. Reactions vary even within the countries of the region. Brazilian agricultural producers are upbeat about the rise of China, while Brazilian manufacturers complain of unfair competition and call for protectionist measures.

This chapter measures the extent to which China might impact LAC countries through heightened competition in world markets[2]. Competition in the US market is especially important because the United States has traditionally been LAC's trading partner *par excellence* as already stressed in Chapters 2 and 3 of this book. Hence the analysis focuses particularly on assessing how international economic policy changes could affect Latin American exports to the United States. The relevance of such an exercise is apparent. The exorbitant US trade deficit with China, which exceeded $200 billion in 2005, has created tension between the two countries. Protectionist feelings against China are hence on the rise in the United States. Amidst an ongoing debate on the underlying nature of the ballooning trade deficit and of global current account imbalances in general, some analysts blame China's exchange-rate policy for keeping its currency, the renminbi (RMB), undervalued. Absent a correction of the Chinese policies that prevent an appreciation of the RMB, US policymakers have proposed slapping surcharges on all Chinese exports to the United States. While RMB appreciation would reduce Chinese exports to the United States, the relative price of exports from the rest of the world would fall, making exports from Latin America and other regions more appealing to US consumers. A key question then is how much Latin American exporters would gain from a revaluation of the Chinese currency.

Another reason to care about assessing the sensitivity of LAC exports to Chinese competition is the emphasis that current US trade policy gives to the pursuit of bilateral trade agreements with Latin American countries. In addition to having free trade agreements in place with Mexico (1994) and Chile (2004), the United States has recently signed an agreement with five Central American countries and the Dominican Republic, has finalised negotiations with Colombia and Peru in 2006, and is currently engaged in talks with the Ecuadorean government. While the political momentum toward establishing a hemisphere-wide free trade area has fizzled, it is worthwhile asking how much the elimination of US tariffs on all Latin American countries might help them compete with Chinese goods in US markets.

Latin American countries have worried particularly about the elimination of import quotas on textile and apparel products, in compliance with the WTO's Agreement on Textiles and Apparel (the Multi-fibre Agreement, or MFA). Import quotas restricted access to US and European markets for Asian exporters. Analysts have argued that Latin American countries, faced with higher labour and energy costs than their Chinese counterparts, would be greatly affected by the elimination of quotas. In January 2002, the third stage in the elimination of quotas was put in place, coinciding with a sharp increase in Chinese apparel exports and a parallel decline in LAC sales to the United States. In January 2005 the fourth and final stage was implemented. Was the decline in LAC exports after 2002 the result of the elimination of quotas? Does the final elimination presage even more trouble for Latin American exporters?

Although changes in the international economic policy environment such as those described above would certainly be expected to tilt the balance between China and Latin America in selling to the United States, exports could also be affected by domestic factors that reduce the ability of Latin American firms to compete in world markets. In marked contrast to China, productivity growth in Latin America has been downright disappointing. That may go far to explain the lethargic export performance of the region. Therefore, the analysis here offers a tentative assessment of the extent to which slow productivity growth may explain Latin America's limited exports.

To assess how Latin American exports would be affected by Chinese competition under each scenario, the chapter relies on the authors' estimates of the elasticity of substitution between imports from different countries in US consumption. López-Córdova et al. (2005) present a technical account of the methodology used for deriving these estimates. The analysis here emphasises their policy applications.

Evolution of Latin American and Chinese Exports to the United States

The United States has been Latin America's most important trade partner in the post-war era. Trade with the United States stood at 60 per cent of the region's trade with the world in 2000[3], up from less than 47 per cent in 1960, having grown continuously since the mid-1970s (Figure 4.1). Latin America has also been an important trade partner for the United States, but with significant fluctuations over the last three decades. As Figure 4.2 shows, total trade with Latin America fell in importance through the late 1980s, but has since picked up. Figure 4.2 also highlights the growing importance of US-China trade, which has risen from an insignificant fraction of US trade to more than 5 per cent currently.

The remarkable growth in US trade with China and the challenges it portends for Latin American countries are most impressive in US import data (Table 4.1). From 1990 to 2003, Latin American exports to the United States increased from $58 billion to $196 billion, growing in real terms at an annual rate of 6.9 per cent. As US imports from the world as a whole grew at 4.8 per cent over the same period, Latin America's share of the US market rose from 13.5 per cent in 1990 to 17.5 per cent in 2003. In the meantime, however, Chinese sales to the United States grew at a breakneck 16.6 per cent annually, reaching $147 billion in 2003. China's export dynamism pushed its share of US imports to increase four-fold to 13.2 per cent in 2003.

Although Latin America as a whole had a fair export performance over the last decade, aggregate figures mask important differences among countries in the region. The lion's share of the increase in exports from Latin America, more than 80 per cent, came from Mexico, which raised its share of the US market from 6 per cent to 11.5 per cent from 1990 to 2003. Over the same period, exports from Caribbean, Andean and other South American countries grew more slowly than world exports to the United States; only Central America, along with Mexico, performed better than the world as whole. Even Mexico, despite being bound to the United States by geography and by the North American Free Trade Agreement (NAFTA), has not been able to keep up with China's export dynamism. By 2003 China had surpassed Mexico as the United States' second most important import supplier, behind Canada.

Aggregate trade figures also hide differences in the sector composition of Chinese and Latin American exports to the United States (Table 4.2). LAC is an important supplier of agricultural and mining products (including oil) to the United States, with shares of around 50 per cent and 30 per cent of US import demand respectively. Close to a quarter of all Latin American exports consist of non-manufactured goods – around three quarters for the Andean countries. At the opposite extreme, Mexico has the highest share of manufactured exports to the United States (86 per cent), followed by Central America and South America (84 per cent in both cases). Central in particular saw a significant change in the composition of its exports. In a shift from

Table 4.1. **Chinese Export-Price Elasticity of US Imports, by Region, 2001**
(Per cent change in US imports from each region in response to a 1 per cent reduction in the prices of Chinese goods)

	Total Trade	Agriculture	Mining	Total	Leather, Apparel, Textiles	Machinery and Equipment	Other
World	0.421	0.040	0.000	0.482	1.024	0.414	0.428
LAC	-0.080	-0.002	-0.001	-0.094	-0.244	-0.085	-0.030
Mexico	-0.084	-0.002	-0/001	-0.093	-0.246	-0.086	-0.046
Central America	-0.104	-0.001	-0.001	-0.129	-0.142	-0.184	-0.035
Caribbean	-0.099	-0.003	-0.002	-0.111	-0.207	-0.107	-0.008
Andean	-0.011	0.000	-0.001	-0.045	-0.185	-0.082	-0.009
South America	-0.110	-0.004	-0.002	-0.097	-0.797	-0.049	-0.015
China	3.690	1.940	0.443	3.679	4.533	3.757	3.021
Rest of the World	-0.074	-0.004	-0.001	-0.082	-0.383	-0.073	-0.027

Source: Authors' calculations.

Table 4.2. **Chinese Revaluation and US Imports, by Region, 2001**
(Per cent change in US imports from each region in response to a 20 per cent RMB revaluation)

	Total Trade	Agriculture	Mining	Total	Leather, Apparel, Textiles	Machinery and Equipment	Other
World	-2.524	-0.239	-0.002	-2.895	-6.145	-2.483	-2.567
LAC	0.478	0.011	0.005	0.566	1.461	0.508	0.181
Mexico	0.507	0.011	0.005	0.555	1.474	0.517	0.279
Central America	0.626	0.003	0.004	0.774	0.852	1.106	0.208
Caribbean	0.592	0.015	0.010	0.667	1.243	0.641	0.050
Andean	0.066	0.002	0.004	0.271	1.111	0.493	0.056
South America	0.660	0.025	0.010	0.584	4.781	0.295	0.091
China	-22.140	-11.641	-2.661	-22.075	-27.198	-22.544	-18.126
Rest of the World	0.444	0.023	0.004	0.490	2.300	0.438	0.163

Source: Authors' calculations.

Figure 4.1. **Latin America's Trade with the United States, 1960-2000**

Note: Total trade is the sum of exports and imports.
Source: Based on IMF data.

Figure 4.2. **US Trade with China and Latin America, 1960-2000**

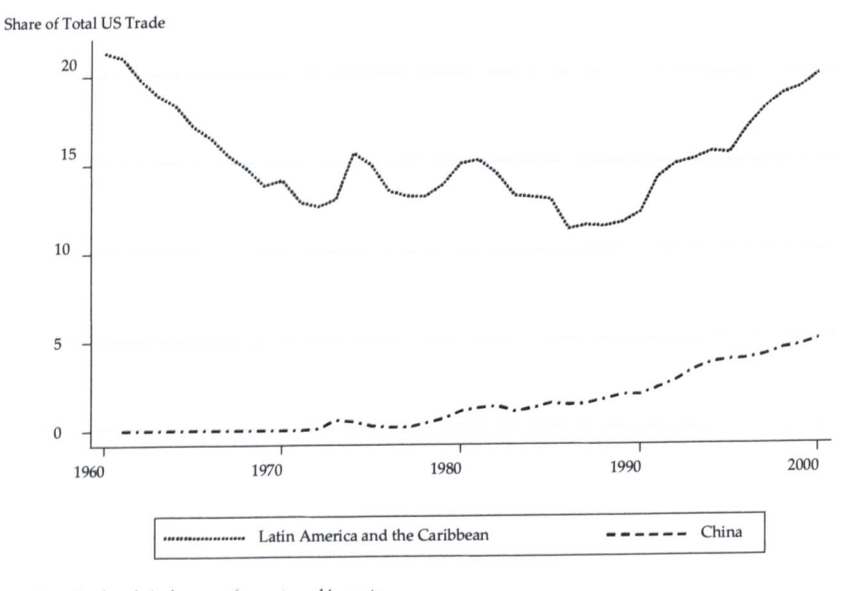

Share of Total US Trade

·········· Latin America and the Caribbean   – – – – – China

Note: Total trade is the sum of exports and imports.
Source: Based on IMF data.

Table 4.3. **Tariff Elimination on Latin American Goods and US Imports, by Region, 2001**
(Per cent change in US imports from each region in response to tariff reduction on Latin American exports to the level of Mexico in 2001)

	Total Trade	Agriculture	Mining	Total	Manufactured Goods Leather, Apparel, Textiles	Machinery and Equipment	Other
World	0.403	0.367	0.004	0.429	3.100	0.104	0.134
LAC	3.055	0.780	0.024	3.693	20.165	0.790	1.275
Mexico	0.801	0.961	0.000	0.836	2.796	0.678	0,599
Central America	20.869	0.000	-0.005	26.966	36.292	0.607	0.000
Caribbean	8.944	-0.126	0.000	9.698	21.117	1.000	0.603
Andean	1.311	-0.016	0.051	5.929	28.845	2.257	0.713
South America	6.360	1.930	0.010	5.700	36.020	2.115	3.185
China	-0.304	-0.031	-0.003	-0.239	-1.098	-0.045	-0.006
Rest of the World	-0.134	-0.020	-0.004	-0.155	-1.695	-0.029	-0.023

Source: Authors' calculations.

agricultural to manufactured exports the share of agricultural exports dropped by 20 percentage points. In contrast with Latin America, China is a relatively insignificant supplier of agricultural and mining exports, while manufactures represent over 99 per cent of its exports to the United States. AmericaImportant differences appear within the manufacturing sector as well (Table 4.3). In 2003, leather (including footwear), textile and apparel products comprised approximately a fifth of all Chinese exports to the US market, compared with 8 per cent to 9 per cent for Mexico and South America and 75 per cent for Central America. Moreover, machinery and equipment exports amounted to almost half of all Chinese sales to the United States compared with 5 per cent and 10 per cent for the Andean and Central American countries, respectively and 76 per cent for Mexico.

China's strong export performance – and Latin America's relative weakness – have become patently manifest since 2000. During 2000-2003, as US demand for world goods declined at a rate of 3.2 per cent per year (2.7 per cent for Latin American goods), Chinese exports to the United States expanded by 11.9 per cent per annum (Table 4.1). The figures for manufacturing are more dismal, showing a yearly drop of 3.9 per cent in overall Latin American exports and declines as high as 12 per cent and 17 per cent, respectively, for the Caribbean and Andean nations (Table 4.3). Chinese exports of leather goods, apparel and textiles climbed by 7.3 per cent annually, compared with negative rates greater than 8 per cent for Mexico and South America; for Latin America as a whole, such exports fell by more than 5 per cent per year. In machinery and equipment, while China's exports grew by 15 per cent annually, exports from Central America contracted at almost 18 per cent per year, although the region as a whole performed slightly better.

China's export dynamism has been undeterred by higher tariffs levied in the United States against it relative to Latin America. In 2003, average tariffs on manufactured imports were more than three times as high on Chinese as on Latin American goods. Mexican exports of leather goods, textiles and apparel paid on average 0.8 per cent *ad valorem*, compared with 9.4 per cent paid on Chinese exports. Of course, averages hide differences in the composition of exports coming from each country and should be read with caution. Still, tariff provisions under NAFTA, the Andean Trade Preference Act (ATPA) or the Caribbean Basin Initiative (CBI) give a preferential edge to some Latin American nations over China. While some studies demonstrate that tariff preferences (e.g. those under NAFTA) indeed have led to increased exports to the United States, China appears to have a comparative advantage that is difficult to compensate through low tariffs on Latin American exports.

One cannot extract causal conclusions regarding the impact of Chinese competition on LAC exports from the previous figures. LAC's modest export performance after 2000 could have resulted from slowdown of the US economy or from internal factors that hinder export competitiveness in the region. Indeed, Hanson and Robertson (2006), looking at Mexico, conclude that China is responsible for just a small fraction of the decline in Mexican sales to the United States, with the lion's share explained by factors that constrain Mexico's own export capacity. Still, China's and Latin America's export baskets are increasingly similar (Devlin *et al.*, 2005), especially for LAC countries that export manufactures, and as a result LAC would be vulnerable to heightened Chinese competition.

The picture that emerges from the foregoing barrage of trade statistics shows that China has become a direct competitor with Latin American countries in their prime export destination, and that such competition may be eroding their share of the US market. That appears to be particularly the case for exporters of manufactures, such as Mexico, Central America and the Caribbean, and especially in low-wage industries, like leather-goods, textiles, and apparel.

A natural question to ask is how changes in the policy environment would alter the current situation. Some of the countries that appear more vulnerable to Chinese competition are in the process of establishing trade agreements granting them preferential access to the US market – e.g. CAFTA[3] – and the region as a whole contemplates a hemispheric-wide *Free Trade Area of the*

Americas (FTAA) agreement. Both might help the region compete more effectively with China in the United States. On the other hand, the January 2005 removal of quotas in place under the MFA presages increased Chinese presence in US apparel and textile consumption[4]. Beyond changes in the realm of trade policy, other factors that come to mind are the potential impact on Latin American exports of renminbi appreciation, or of China continuing to outpace Latin America in productivity growth.

Estimating the Sensitivity of LAC Exports to Chinese competition

The analysis here of how LAC competes with Chinese products in the US market first computes US import elasticities. Assume that there is a set of goods and that each country can produce a different variety of each good. For goods produced in a given sector, US imports are characterised by a constant elasticity of substitution (CES) demand function. The flexible specification used allows different preferences for each good and variety. It also allows preferences for goods from a given country as well as the US expenditure share in each sector to vary over time. López-Córdova *et al.* (2005) present a complete description of the empirical framework. The import elasticities are computed using a two-stage least squares approach and bilateral US import data for 1990-2003. The US Customs data are disaggregated at the 6-digit harmonised system level and cover imports from more than 150 countries around the world.

Assuming that all sectors have the same elasticity of substitution, the estimates suggest that the within-sector US import demand elasticity is around five. This lies in the range of previous studies – in the lower bound of Romalis (2003) for Mexico, for example. The assumption that the elasticity of substitution is constant across sectors is rather strong, however. Contrary to previous papers[5], the methodology permits relaxing that assumption. The results presented below assume different within-sector elasticities, which are computed for five different sectors (agriculture, mining, textiles, fabricated metal products, machinery and equipment and other manufacturing products). The results reported in López-Córdova *et al.* (2005) show that within manufacturing, textiles products have a significantly larger elasticity of substitution (seven). For agriculture the elasticity is three whereas it is almost seven for mining, consistent with what one should expect for such a commodity sector. To summarise, within-sector elasticities vary significantly across sectors, and it is important to consider such heterogeneity in estimating the potential effect of any change in trade policies on bilateral trade flows.

What do the elasticity estimates tell us about China-LAC competition? Table 4.1 (see also Annex on page 128) presents forecast estimates of how a one per cent drop in the price of Chinese exports to the United States affects sales to US consumers, from both China and the rest of the world. Naturally, a price drop leads to an expansion of Chinese exports to the United States, by 3.7 per cent according to these results, while exports from other regions fall. Sales from Latin America and the rest of the world decline by 0.1 per cent each. Overall US imports increase by a mere 0.3 per cent. As expected, the biggest impact occurs in the manufacturing sector, where China's export offer is concentrated. Chinese exports of leather goods, apparel and textiles rise by 4.5 per cent, drastically displacing exports from Mexico (0.2 per cent) and South America (0.8 per cent). Machinery and equipment sales from Central America decline by 0.2 per cent as they are displaced by a 3.8 per cent increase in Chinese exports.

Policy Scenarios

Consider now how exports to the United States from LAC, China and the rest of the world may change under alternative policy scenarios. Three such scenarios are constructed – for a revaluation of the RMB, for an elimination of US tariffs on imports from Latin America, and for the ending of US quotas on textile imports from China – the latter two being US trade policy variants. Finally, the analysis looks at productivity growth differentials as determinant of lagging export performance in Latin America. The methodology for computing such forecasts is described in López-Córdova *et al.* (2005).

Currency Revaluation

One can apply the elasticities in Table 4.1 to an assessment of the potential implications for US imports of a revaluation of the Chinese currency. The analysis is admittedly crude, as it assumes that exchange-rate appreciation leads only to changes in the prices of Chinese goods with no general equilibrium effects on either the Chinese economy or the rest of the world. Indeed, it assumes that the exchange rates of other countries remain unchanged, which is probably a strong assumption, especially regarding other Asian nations. Potential adverse effects of the revaluation on the Chinese economy, such as disruptions in the financial sector, also are ignored.

Consider what would happen if the RMB is revalued by 20 per cent. This does not imply that the prices of Chinese exports increase by the same percentage. Chinese exports embody a large fraction of imported inputs – as much as 70 per cent of the value of exports, according to some authors. Taking that figure as valid and assuming that a revaluation increases only the prices of Chinese inputs, including labour, embodied in exports (30 per cent of their value) a 20 per cent revaluation implies a 6 per cent increase in the price of Chinese exports. Table 4.2 (see also Annex on page 128) shows the forecasts for US imports under this scenario.

These estimates suggest that a 20 per cent RMB revaluation would reduce Chinese exports to the United States by more than a fifth, or $54 billion based on 2005 trade figures. Chinese sales of leather products, apparel and textiles would be the most sensitive, falling by close to 27 per cent. Importantly, such a renminbi revaluation would have only a modest impact on total US imports, which would decline by a mere 2.5 per cent ($42 billion). Since the US current account deficit in 2005 exceeded $200 billion, the view that a relaxation of China's exchange-rate policy would provide the silver bullet to correct US external imbalances is probably misplaced. Solving global imbalances requires a multi-dimensional strategy, involving perhaps greater RMB flexibility in addition to greater economic dynamism in Europe and a fiscal adjustment in the United States.

A change in China's exchange-rate policy would not reduce US imports significantly because, as one would expect, an RMB appreciation would result in improved export competitiveness in the rest of the world. In particular, Latin American sales to the United States would grow by 0.5 per cent or close to $1.4 billion from the 2005 level. While South and Central American countries would benefit most, the Andean countries would see marginal increases in exports due to the prominence of oil in their export baskets. Exports of leather, apparel and textiles from this region would grow by 1.5 per cent – 4.8 per cent for South America. Thus, the message emerges that just as the United States should not view a revaluation in China as a solution to its trade imbalances, Latin America should not expect it to boost sales to the US market significantly.

Elimination of US Tariffs on Latin American Goods

What would a reduction in US tariffs on Latin American goods mean for the region's exports? This question arises because since 1994, when the United States adopted NAFTA, it has engaged in negotiations with other countries in the region to establish similar free-trade agreements. In 2004 it approved an FTA with Chile; it recently finished negotiating CAFTA and is holding negotiations with Andean nations on similar agreements.

Table 4.3 (see also Annex on page 128) considers the elimination of US 2003 tariffs on imports from all of LAC. In the aggregate, LAC exports increase by 3 per cent, although there is wide variation among the different sub-regions. The biggest increase would take place in Central America, with shipments to the United States expanding by 21 per cent, driven largely by increased sales of leather goods, apparel and textiles, which grow by 36 per cent. Indeed, for almost all of LAC such exports would grow the fastest: 21 per cent for the Caribbean, 29 per cent for the Andean countries and 36 per cent for South America. The smallest increase would come from Mexico, which by 2003 had seen tariffs on its exports to the United States drastically reduced as a result of NAFTA.

These forecasts fall in line with others. For example, a United States International Trade Commission report (USITC, 2004) analysing the potential impact of CAFTA on trade patterns estimates that US imports from the five Central American counterparts in the agreement (Costa Rica, El Salvador, Guatemala, Honduras, and Nicaragua) and from the Dominican Republic would increase by 26 per cent, which falls within the forecast here for the Caribbean and Central America. With an FTAA, Hertel *et al.* (2004) estimate that total US imports would rise by around 2.2 per cent, whereas Watanuki and Monteagudo (2002) put the figure at 1.1 per cent; in contrast, the estimate here foresees an increase of only 0.4 per cent.

The results here highlight the importance of preferential trade between the United States and Latin America for boosting exports from the region. The flip side reveals small reductions in exports from China and the rest of the world to the United States of around 0.3 per cent and 0.1 per cent, respectively. The largest declines, as expected, would occur in exports of leather, apparel and textiles, and in manufacturing in general. While the decline in exports from China and the rest of the world should raise concerns about the trade-diverting effects of free trade agreements, the increase in overall US imports (by 0.4 per cent) suggests that an FTAA would create enough trading opportunities to offset any trade diversion.

ISBN: 9789264027961

Table 4.4. US Apparel Imports and Average Tariffs, by Origin

	Volume ($ million)			Regional Distribution (per cent)				Average Tariffs (per cent)			
	1997	2000	2003	2004	1997	2000	2003	2004	1997	2000	2003	2004
World	47 084	62 928	66 499	70 533	100.0	100.0	100.0	100.0	12.6	12.1	11.2	10.9
LAC	13 669	19 376	18 150	18 517	29.0	30.8	27.3	26.3	5.6	5.5	3.4	3.3
Mexico	5 317	8 704	7 178	6 930	11.3	13.8	10.8	9.8	1.0	0.4	0.7	0.7
Central America	4 781	6 702	7 159	7 560	10.2	10.7	10.8	10.7	8.9	9.9	6.0	6.0
Caribbean	2 871	2 987	2 540	2 481	6.1	4.7	3.8	3.5	6.9	7.5	2.5	2.3
Andean	575	844	1 062	1 331	1.2	1.3	1.6	1.9	13.1	14.7	4.1	1.8
South America	125	140	211	215	0.3	0.2	0.3	0.3	10.3	12.9	14.1	12.3
China	7 279	8 307	10 997	13 106	15.5	13.2	16.5	18.6	11.8	10.5	10.0	9.5
Rest of the World	26 136	35 245	37 352	38 909	55.5	56.0	56.2	55.2	16.6	16.1	15.3	14.9

Note: Average tariffs are calculated duties divided by the value of imports.

Source: US Customs data, authors' calculations.

Elimination of Textile Quotas:

Latin American countries probably have felt the brunt of Chinese competition in the textile and apparel sector. As Table 4.4 shows, whereas from 2000 to 2004 China's share of US apparel imports rose from 13.2 per cent to 18.6 per cent, Latin America's participation in the US market declined from 30.8 per cent to 26.3 per cent. China's increasing market share and Latin America's loss came despite a greater decline in US tariffs on imports from LAC than in those on Chinese goods. One potential explanation for the rising presence of Chinese apparel during this period was the elimination in 2002 of a number of import quotas on textile and apparel imports under the MFA. MFA quotas binding on China and other Asian nations limited market access on apparel exports from those countries. During the Uruguay Round, countries agreed to dismantle such quotas gradually, removing them altogether by 1 January 2005. The recent implementation of the final stage of quota elimination in the United States and elsewhere has created widespread apprehension in Latin America that unfettered Chinese exports to the United States will continue to erode the region's exports to the US market.

Previous studies that tried to predict the impact of MFA quota elimination on Latin American exports offered gloomy prospects for the region. For example, Nordas (2004) found that China's share of the US apparel market would jump from 16 per cent to 50 per cent; in contrast, Mexico's share would fall from 10 per cent to 3 per cent, and that of the rest of Latin America from 16 per cent to 5 per cent. Does the elasticity-based methodology yield similarly negative predictions? To apply this framework to the analysis of the potential impact that MFA quota elimination might have on exports to the United States requires some measure of how much the relative price of Chinese and LAC exports would change without quotas. To that end, one can use available estimates of the export tariff equivalents of the quotas and apply the estimated elasticities of substitution to understand the implications of the ensuing relative price changes. According to USITC (2002), the export tariff equivalent of the quota for Chinese apparel sales to the United States was approximately 21 per cent. In estimating the elasticities of substitution, López-Córdova et al. (2005) assume that all Chinese apparel exports were subject to this export tariff equivalent in addition to the usual duties applied in the United States.

Column one of Table 4.5 presents the forecasts of the impact of quota elimination on US imports. Chinese exports increase by an impressive 75 per cent, paralleled by falls everywhere else. US imports grow by a modest 2.2 per

Table 4.5. **Elimination of MFA Quotas and US Apparel Imports, by Region, 2003**

	Using Elasticities of Substitution		Based on Difference-in-Difference Results	
	Imports (% change)	Market Share Change (percentage points)	Market Share Change (percentage points)	P-value of Point Estimate
World	2.2	0.0	--	--
LAC	-7.7	-2.6	-2.5	0.3
Mexico	-8.2	-1.1	-2.2	0.3
Central America	-7.0	-1.0	-1.8	0.3
Caribbean	-7.8	-0.4	-0.3	0.8
Andean	-7.3	-0.1	0.4	0.4
South America	-17.0	-0.1	-0.6	0.4
China	74.9	11.8	25.3	0.0
Rest of the World	-14.4	-9.1	-24.4	0.0

Source: Authors' calculations.

cent. Latin America is undeniably affected, but the forecasts are smaller than in the apparent common perception – between 7 per cent and 8 per cent, except for 17 per cent for South America. Column 2 shows what the forecasts imply for the change (in percentage points) in each region's share of the US market. China's share rises by 11.8 points, Latin America's falls by 2.7 points, and the rest of the world accounts for the balance.

Because these results clearly contrast with previous findings, one must assess whether they are reasonable. An alternative strategy to measure the impact of removing quotas on each region's market participation employs a difference-in-differences approach to compare changes in market shares from 2000 to 2003 in tariff lines that had import quotas removed in 2002 (the treatment group), with those in tariff lines that had quotas eliminated in 2005 (the control group); see Appendix C in López-Córdova et al. (2005) for details. Columns three and four of Table 4.5 present the findings alongside the previous elasticity-based results. For Latin America and the Caribbean, these point estimates are remarkably similar to the previous findings – a market-share loss of around 2.5 percentage points – although one cannot reject the null hypothesis that the impact on market share is zero, which is true for all sub-regions of Latin America. In contrast, the estimates for China and the rest of the world are substantially higher (in absolute terms). Overall, the difference-in-differences approach suggests that Chinese market-share gains have come mainly not at the expense of Latin America, but at the rest of the world's. Even if the impact is small, the recent adoption of safeguard measures against Chinese exports to the United States should give a respite to LAC countries in the face of Chinese competition[6].

Productivity Growth and Chinese Exports

So far the different scenarios have shown that the relative under-performance of Latin America *vis-à-vis* China in exporting to the US market has little to do with any under-appreciation of the renminbi or with increased access to the US market for Chinese products that might have resulted from the elimination of MFA quotas. Moreover, whereas US tariff preferences in the context of a regional trade agreement would help Latin American exports compete with China and other countries, Latin America should not rely on preferential access as a long-term solution to its competitiveness challenges. Mexico, which gained market access to the United States under NAFTA in 1994 but has recently seen its tariff advantage erode, should serve as an example.

Latin American countries should give special attention to productivity growth as a way to sustain export dynamism. Improvements in productivity allow a country to produce goods at lower cost and consequently to compete more effectively in world markets. Unfortunately, Latin America has lagged in this area; the challenge it faces becomes evident in comparison with China. China's productivity performance has been impressive since it embarked on economic liberalisation. Annual TFP growth estimates range from as low as 1.4 per cent to as high as 4 per cent (Moreira, 2004). In contrast, Latin America's productivity growth has been modest if not rather disappointing. During the 1980s and 1990s, TFP growth was negative for the region as a whole (Loayza *et al.*, 2002). López-Córdova and Moreira (2004) estimate TFP growth in the late 1990s at 1.1 per cent for Mexico and 2.7 per cent for Brazil.

In light of the sharp differences in productivity performance between China and Latin America, it is reasonable to ask to what extent poor productivity growth in LAC may explain the increasing gap in export performance of the two regions. Although offering a rigorous answer to that question is beyond the capabilities of the methodology here, one can venture a back-of-the-envelope calculation. Between 2000 and 2003, the annual difference in the growth rates of US manufactured imports from China and Latin America equalled 15.9 percentage points. Assume that the gap in productivity growth between China and Latin America from 2000 to 2003 continued at around two percentage points per year and that each point in TFP growth translates one-to-one into declines of export prices. Then, the results in Table 4.6 would suggest that faster productivity growth in China accounts for 7.4 percentage points – or slightly less than one-half – of the difference in the annual growth rates of exports to the United States[7]. A similar

Table 4.6. **China-Latin America Productivity Growth Differentials and US Imports by Region, 2001**
(Change in US imports from a 2 per cent TFP growth gap between China and Latin America)

	Total Trade	Agriculture	Mining	Manufacturing Total	Leather. Apparel, Textiles	Machinery and Equipment	Other
World	0.841	0.080	0.001	0.965	2.048	0.828	0.856
LAC	-0.159	-0.004	-0.002	-0.189	-0.487	-0.169	-0.060
Mexico	-0.169	-0.004	-0.002	-0.185	-0.491	-0.172	-0.093
Central America	-0.209	-0.001	-0.001	-0.258	-0.284	-0.369	-0.069
Caribbean	-0.197	-0.005	-0.003	-0.222	-0.414	-0.214	-0.017
Andean	-0.022	-0.001	-0.001	-0.090	-0.370	-0.164	-0.019
South America	-0.220	-0.008	-0.003	-0.195	-1.594	-0.098	-0.030
China	7.380	3.880	0.887	7.358	9.066	7.515	6.042
Rest of the World	-0.148	-0.008	-0.001	-0.163	-0.797	-0.146	-0.054

Source: Authors' calculations.

exercise for the leather, apparel and textiles sector suggests that 9.1 points of the 12.4 percentage-point gap between Chinese and Latin American exports are explained by faster productivity growth in China.

Although this exercise is rather rough and demands careful interpretation, it stresses the need for countries in the region to embark on an introspective examination of the factors that may be holding back productivity growth. Latin American countries consistently trail other regions in the integrity of their institutions, in the quality and availability of their infrastructure, in R&D spending and in the number of available skilled workers. These are among the factors that the region must address in order to participate successfully in world markets and compete effectively with China and other countries.

Final Remarks

China's rise in world markets has been a source of apprehension in Latin America. While its sheer size and labour abundance make China a formidable competitor, the scenarios considered here suggest that Latin American countries should not expect changes in economic policies at the international level to give a big and long-lasting boost to their ability to compete in world markets. First, although a large appreciation of the renminbi (by 20 per cent) would have a significant impact on Chinese sales to the United States, reducing exports by more than one-fifth, Latin American exports would increase by only 0.5 per cent. Moreover, in a by-product of the analysis, the impact on overall US imports would be modest so that a revaluation of the Chinese currency would not significantly dent US external imbalances in the absence of additional changes in the international economy. Second, the removal of MFA quotas would lead to a sharp increase in Chinese sales to the United States (75 per cent), but Latin America would see its share of the US market decline by only around 10 per cent (2.5 percentage points). China's gains would come mainly at the expense of other regions of the world. Third, hemispheric free trade would increase Latin America's exports to the United States by around 3 per cent, with an especially significant impact on Central American exports (a 21 per cent increase). Nonetheless, to the extent that the United States negotiates trade agreements with others (e.g. Thailand) or that it further reduces MFN tariffs, tariff preferences represent no long-term remedy for Latin America's modest export performance. Last, a rough calculation suggests that lagging productivity growth is a main culprit for the region's poor export performance. It explains about half of the gap in export growth between China and Latin America in recent years. In light of all these findings, stress should go on the importance of addressing the factors that may affect Latin America's productivity performance.

Notes

1. Ernesto López-Córdova is an economist at the Inter-American Development Bank (IDB); Alejandro Micco was at the time of writing an economist in the IDB Research Department and later with the Banco Central de Chile; Danielken Molina is an economist from the University of California at San Diego. The opinions expressed herein are those of the authors and do not necessarily reflect the views of the IDB or the Banco Central de Chile.

2. See Devlin *et al*. (2005).

3. "Trade" here means the sum of imports and exports.

4. The US-Dominican Republic-Central America Free Trade Agreement.

5. In November 2005 the United States adopted safeguards on Chinese textile products. The safeguards will be in effect through 2008.

6. In his paper Romalis (2004) states that "...there is insufficient tariff variation to obtain meaningful substitution elasticity estimates for detailed industries."

7. See endnote 5.

The Visible Hand of China in Latin America

Table A4.1. **US Imports and Average Tariffs, by Origin**

	Volume ($ millions)			US Imports Distribution (Per cent)			Annual Real Growth Rate (Per cent)			Average Tariffs (Per cent)		
	1990	2000	2003	1990	2000	2003	1990-2000	1990-2003	2000-2003	1990	2000	2003
World	431 318	1 153 203	1 116 347	100.0	100.0	100.0	7.3	4.8	-3.2	4.6	2.5	2.1
LAC	58 286	198 906	195 848	13.5	17.3	17.5	10.0	6.9	-2.7	3.0	1.3	0.8
Mexico	25 872	124 408	128 430	6.0	11.1	11.5	14.2	10.2	-2.2	2.8	0.8	0.4
Central America	2 704	11 824	11 654	0.6	1.0	1.0	12.7	9.0	-2.7	5.0	5.2	4.4
Caribbean	4 494	9 770	9 913	1.0	0.8	0.8	5.1	2.9	-4.1	4.9	3.3	2.2
Andean	14 670	29 295	25 011	3.4	2.5	2.2	4.2	1.5	-7.2	1.4	0.7	0.5
South America	10 546	19 609	21 560	2.4	1.7	1.9	3.5	2.9	1.0	4.3	2.4	1.6
China	14 254	98 267	146 989	3.3	8.5	13.2	18.0	16.6	11.9	7.8	4.7	3.6
Rest of World	358 778	855 030	773 510	83.2	74.2	69.3	6.1	3.3	-5.4	4.7	2.6	2.2

Notes: Annual real growth calculated using US CPI as deflator. Average tariffs are calculated duties divided by the value of imports
Source: Authors' calculations based on US Customs data.

ISBN: 9789264027961

Competing with the Dragon: Latin American and Chinese Exports to the US Market

Table A4.2. US Imports and Average Tariffs, by Origin and Sector

	Volume ($ million)			US Imports						Annual Real Growth (Per cent)			Average Tariffs (Per cent)		
				Regional Distribution (Per cent)			As Per cent of Imports from Region								
	1990	2000	2003	1990	2000	2003	1990	2000	2003	1990-2000	1990-2003	2000-2003	1990	2000	2003
Agriculture															
World	10 350	17 621	18 266	100.0	100.0	100.0	2.4	1.5	1.6	2.6	1.8	-1.0	3.6	1.4	0.7
LAC	5 243	8 499	8 848	50.7	48.2	48.4	9.0	4.3	4.5	2.1	1.4	-0.9	2.9	0.6	0.3
Mexico	1 873	3 152	3 491	18.1	17.9	19.1	7.2	2.5	2.7	2.5	2.2	1.2	5.2	0.6	0.2
Central America	988	1 820	1 706	9.6	10.3	9.3	36.6	15.4	14.6	3.4	1.6	-4.3	0.7	0.1	0.1
Caribbean	142	163	170	1.4	0.9	0.9	3.2	1.7	1.8	-1.4	-1.3	-0.9	0.6	0.0	0.0
Andean	1 188	1 611	1 622	11.5	9.1	8.9	8.1	5.5	6.5	0.3	-0.2	-2.0	2.2	0.2	0.1
South America	1 052	1 173	1 860	10.2	9.9	10.2	10.0	8.9	8.6	2.4	1.8	-0.2	2.1	1.6	0.7
China	105	298	401	1.0	1.7	2.2	0.7	0.3	0.3	8.0	8.0	8.0	2.4	28.5	1.8
Rest of the World	5 003	8 824	9 017	48.3	50.1	49.4	1.4	1.0	1.2	3.0	1.9	-1.5	4.3	1.2	1.0
Mining															
World	49 326	104 516	126 384	100.0	100.0	100.0	11.4	9.1	11.3	4.9	4.7	4.2	0.3	1.2	0.0
LAC	13 100	31 523	36 311	26.6	30.2	28.7	22.5	15.8	18.5	6.2	5.3	2.5	0.2	0.1	0.0
Mexico	5 064	12 116	14 589	10.3	11.6	11.5	19.6	9.4	11.4	6.1	5.7	4.1	0.2	0.0	0.0
Central America	25	154	181	0.1	0.1	0.1	0.9	1.3	1.6	16.6	13.3	3.2	0.3	0.3	0.0
Caribbean	782	980	2 735	1.6	0.9	2.2	17.4	10.0	29.8	-0.5	7.3	37.7	0.2	0.0	0.0
Andean	6 912	17 325	17 110	14.0	16.6	13.5	47.1	59.1	68.4	6.6	4.4	-2.6	0.3	0.2	0.0
South America	318	948	1 696	0.6	0.9	1.3	3.0	4.8	7.9	8.5	10.8	18.8	0.4	0.1	0.1
China	725	608	329	1.5	0.6	0.3	5.1	0.6	0.2	-4.4	-8.3	-20.2	0.7	0.2	0.3
Rest of the World	35 501	72 385	89 743	72.0	69.3	71.0	9.9	8.5	11.6	4.5	4.6	5.1	0.3	1.7	0.0
Manufacturing															
World	371 642	1 030 066	971 697	100.0	100.0	100.0	86.2	89.4	87.0	7.7	4.9	-4.1	5.2	2.7	2.4
LAC	39 943	158 884	150 689	10.7	15.4	15.5	68.5	79.9	76.9	11.7	7.9	-3.9	3.9	1.6	1.1
Mexico	18 935	113 140	110 351	5.1	11.0	11.4	73.2	88.1	85.9	16.3	11.5	-3.0	3.3	0.9	0.4
Central America	1 690	9 849	9 767	0.5	1.0	1.0	62.5	83.3	83.8	16.0	11.5	-2.5	7.6	6.2	5.2
Caribbean	3 570	8 627	6 288	1.0	0.8	0.6	79.4	88.3	68.4	6.2	1.7	-12.0	6.1	3.7	3.2
Andean	6 571	10 359	6 279	1.8	1.0	0.6	44.8	35.4	25.1	1.8	-2.9	-17.2	2.5	1.7	1.8
South America	9 177	16 980	18 004	2.5	1.6	1.9	87.0	86.2	83.5	3.4	2.6	-0.1	4.6	2.6	1.8
China	13 424	97 361	146 259	3.6	9.5	15.1	94.2	99.1	99.5	18.6	17.0	12.0	8.2	4.6	3.6
Rest of the World	318 274	773 822	674 749	85.6	75.1	69.4	88.7	90.5	87.2	6.3	3.2	-6.5	5.2	2.7	2.5

Notes: Annual real growth rates calculated using the US CPI as deflator. Average tariffs are calculated duties divided by the value of imports.
Source: Authors' calculations based on US Customs data.

ISBN: 9789264027961

129

Table A4.3. **US Manufactured Goods Imports and Average Tariffs, by Origin and Industry**

	Volume ($ million)			Regional Distribution (%)			% of Manufactured Imports			Annual Real Growth (Per cent)			Average Tariffs (Per cent)		
	1990	2000	2003	1990	2000	2003	1990	2000	2003	1990-2000	1990-2003	2000-2003	1990	2000	2003
Textiles and Apparel															
World	43 417	97 872	102 232	100.0	100.0	100.0	11.7	9.5	10.5	5.5	4.0	-0.7	12.9	10.3	8.7
LAC	5 678	23 742	21 662	13.1	24.3	21.2	14.2	14.9	14.4	12.2	8.0	-5.1	13.0	6.0	4.6
Mexico	1 211	18 810	8 907	2.8	11.0	8.7	6.4	9.6	8.1	21.1	13.6	-8.3	12.0	2.4	0.8
Central America	876	6 806	7 241	2.0	7.0	7.1	51.8	69.1	74.1	19.4	14.6	-0.1	14.0	8.7	6.8
Caribbean	1 362	3 249	2 769	3.1	3.3	2.7	38.1	37.7	44.0	6.1	2.9	-7.3	13.8	8.5	6.5
Andean	375	952	1 147	0.9	1.0	1.1	5.7	9.2	18.3	6.8	6.1	4.1	14.5	10.6	10.0
South America	1 854	1 925	1 598	4.3	2.0	1.6	20.2	11.4	8.9	-2.4	-3.7	-8.1	12.1	10.6	10.0
China	6 319	21 710	28 680	14.6	22.2	28.0	47.1	22.3	19.6	10.1	9.4	7.3	11.6	11.8	9.4
Rest of the World	31 420	52 420	51 990	72.4	53.6	50.8	9.9	6.8	7.7	2.4	1.2	-2.4	13.1	11.5	10.1
Machinery and Equipment															
World	193 344	611 125	563 178	100.0	100.0	100.0	52.0	59.3	58.0	9.1	5.8	-4.8	4.2	1.6	1.3
LAC	15 227	93 195	92 528	7.9	15.2	16.4	38.1	58.7	61.4	16.6	11.9	-2.4	2.6	0.7	0.4
Mexico	12 470	85 640	83 570	6.4	14.0	14.8	65.9	75.7	75.7	17.9	12.8	-3.0	2.7	0.7	0.4
Central America	90	1 602	954	0.0	0.3	0.2	5.3	16.3	9.8	29.8	16.8	-17.7	1.9	0.4	0.5
Caribbean	283	881	970	0.1	0.1	0.2	7.9	10.2	15.4	9.0	7.1	1.0	2.0	0.5	0.5
Andean	189	345	315	0.1	0.1	0.1	2.9	3.3	5.0	3.3	1.3	-5.0	1.6	0.6	0.6
South America	2 196	4 728	6 719	1.1	0.8	1.2	23.9	28.0	37.3	5.0	6.2	10.0	1.8	0.6	0.6
China	2 517	44 330	71 850	1.3	7.3	12.8	18.7	45.4	49.1	29.6	26.0	14.9	5.1	2.3	1.9
Rest of the World	175 600	473 600	398 800	90.8	77.5	70.8	55.2	61.2	59.1	7.4	3.7	-7.6	4.3	1.7	1.5
Other Manufacturing															
World	134 881	321 069	306 187	100.0	100.0	100.0	36.3	31.2	31.5	6.1	3.7	-3.7	4.1	2.4	2.3
LAC	19 039	41 946	36 499	14.1	13.1	11.9	47.7	26.4	24.2	5.2	2.4	-6.6	2.3	1.2	0.7
Mexico	5 254	16 690	17 874	3.9	5.2	5.8	27.7	14.8	16.2	9.2	7.0	0.1	2.7	0.9	0.3
Central America	725	1 441	1 572	0.5	0.4	0.5	42.9	14.6	16.1	4.2	3.4	0.7	0.6	1.1	0.7
Caribbean	1 925	4 497	2 549	1.4	1.4	0.8	53.9	52.1	40.5	5.9	-0.5	-19.0	1.2	0.9	0.6
Andean	6 007	9 062	4 817	4.5	2.8	1.6	91.4	87.5	76.7	1.4	-4.2	-20.8	1.8	0.8	0.6
South America	5 127	10 255	9 687	3.8	3.2	3.2	55.9	60.7	53.8	4.3	2.3	-4.0	3.1	2.1	1.4
China	4 588	31 321	45 729	3.4	9.8	14.9	34.2	32.2	31.3	17.9	16.2	11.0	5.3	2.9	2.8
Rest of the World	111 254	247 802	223 959	82.5	77.2	73.1	35.0	32.0	33.2	5.4	2.8	-5.4	4.4	2.6	2.5

Notes: Annual real growth rates are calculated using the US CPI as deflator. Average tariffs are calculated duties divided by the value of imports.
Source: Authors' calculations based on US Customs data.

Bibliography

DEVLIN, R., A. ESTEVADEORDAL AND A. RODRÍGUEZ (eds.) (2005), *The Emergence of China: Opportunities and Challenges for Latin America and the Caribbean*, Inter-American Development Bank, Washington, D.C., March.

HANSON, G. AND R. ROBERTSON (2006), "The Evolution of Mexico's Manufacturing Exports: A Gravity Framework for Evaluating Supply and Demand Factors", Paper commissioned by the Inter-American Development Bank, Washington, D.C., February.

HERTEL, T., D. HUMMELS, M. IVANIC AND R. KEENEY (2004), "How Confident Can We Be in CGE-Based Assessments of Free Trade Agreements?", Global Trade Analysis Project (GTAP) Working Paper, 26 March, Department of Agricultural Economics, Purdue University, West Lafayette, IN.

LOAYZA, N., P. FAJNZYLBER AND C. CALDERÓN (2002), "Economic Growth in Latin America and the Caribbean: Stylized Facts, Explanations and Forecasts", processed, World Bank, Washington, D.C.

LÓPEZ-CÓRDOVA, E. AND M.M. MOREIRA (2004), "Regional Integration and Productivity: The Experiences of Brazil and Mexico", in A. ESTEVADEORDAL, D. RODRICK, A.M. TAYLOR AND A. VELASCO (eds.), *Integrating the Americas: FTAA and Beyond*, David Rockefeller Center for Latin American Studies, Harvard University Press, Cambridge, MA, chapter 17, pp. 573-609.

LÓPEZ-CÓRDOVA, E., A. MICCO AND D. MOLINA (2005) "How Sensitive are Latin American Exports to Chinese Competition in the U.S. Market?", mimeo, Inter-American Development Bank, Washington, D.C.

MOREIRA, M.M. (2004), "Fear of China: Is There a Future For Manufacturing in Latin America?", Working Paper 33, Latin America/Caribbean and Asia/Pacific Economics and Business Association (LAEBA), Decembe,r paper presented at the 2004 LAEBA Annual Conference, Beijing, PR China, 3-4 December.

NORDAS, H.K. (2004), "The Global Textile and Clothing Industry post the Agreement on Textiles and Clothing", mimeo, World Trade Organization, Geneva.

Romalis, J. (2003), "NAFTA's and CUSFTA's Impact on North American Trade", Graduate School of Business, University of Chicago, December (unpublished).

US International Trade Commission (USITC) (2002), *The Economic Effects of Significant U.S. Import Restraints*, Third Update, USITC Publication 3717, June, Investigation No. 332-325, Publication 3519, USITC, Washington, D.C.

USITC (2004), *U.S.-Central America-Dominican Republic Free Trade Agreement: Potential Economywide and Selected Sectoral Effects*, USITC Publication 3717, Investigation No. TA-2104-13, August, USITC, Washington, D.C.

Watanuki, M. and J. Monteagudo (2002), "FTAA in Perspective: North-South and South-South Agreements in the Western Hemispheric Countries", unpublished manuscript presented at the 5th Annual Conference on Global Economic Analysis, Taipei, Chinese Taipei.

Chapter 5

Does China Have an Impact on Foreign Direct Investment to Latin America?

by Alicia Garcia-Herrero and Daniel Santabárbera[1]

Abstract

This chapter analyses empirically whether the emergence of China as a large recipient of FDI has affected the amount of FDI received by Latin American countries. For the longest possible period given data availability (1984-2001), it finds no diversion of FDI from Latin America to China when other relevant factors are taken into account. Concentrating on the last few years (1995-2001), however, when FDI boomed worldwide and negotiations for China's WTO membership accelerated, the "Chinese effect" becomes highly significant. Assessing the impact country by country, China's inward FDI appears to have hampered that of Mexico and Colombia, but not the other four large Latin American economies studied.

Introduction

The rapid, remarkable emergence of China as an important player in the global economy has consequences for the rest of the world. An important one involves foreign direct investment (FDI). China has attracted a growing share of FDI flows since the1990s. After reaching an average of $28 billion a year in that decade, China's average annual FDI inflows increased to $47 billion after the PRC acceded to the World Trade Organization (WTO) in 2001[2] (Figure 5.1) and continued to grow even faster, reaching $61 billion in 2004. In a relatively short time, China has accumulated the world's third largest stock of inward FDI after the United States and the United Kingdom. Foreign firms are attracted by China's rapid economic growth, increasing demand for consumer goods, relatively skilled and educated workforce for the wages paid, improved infrastructure and more predictable business environment. Since the early 1980s, China has drawn significant investment from regional conglomerates in Hong Kong China, Chinese Taipei, Macao China and Singapore, as well as from the largest industrial economies, particularly Japan and the United States.

Just as many countries fear China as an export competitor, concern grows, especially in developing countries, that FDI may be diverted into China. FDI is very important for Latin America as the major source of external financing that has helped modernise the economic structure. Nonetheless, FDI flows to Latin America started to fall in 2000 while FDI to China has been accelerating (Figure 5.1). Given FDI's relevance for the future of the region, deeper knowledge of its determinants seems clearly warranted. This study focuses on the impact of China as an increasingly important recipient of FDI.

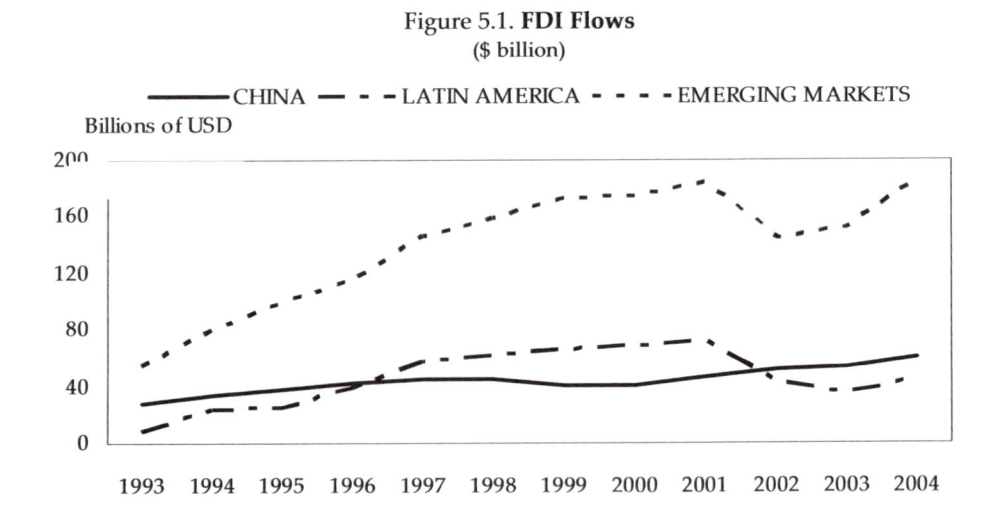

Figure 5.1. **FDI Flows**
($ billion)

Source: Customs Administration of China, WEO database of the IMF.

Whether external financing is diverted from Latin American countries into China will depend on several factors. The first is the degree of integration of capital markets. If they are not fully integrated across countries – or, more likely, regions – an increase in Chinese inward FDI will not necessarily imply a reduction of FDI in other countries or regions. The large regional FDI flows in Asia may fit into this description. In fact, Hong Kong China, Chinese Taipei, Macao China and Singapore have been the main suppliers of FDI to China while practically irrelevant for other parts of the world, including Latin America.

A second factor concerns whether the global supply of FDI is constant or, more specifically, whether China's inward FDI affects worldwide FDI flows. If supply were constant, an increase in FDI to China would reduce the FDI to other regions. This could be the case for Latin America, but not necessarily since other regions could be affected. Moreover, the global supply of FDI may be elastic; in fact, if foreign direct investors reap large benefits from their presence in China or there are spillovers in other countries, more savings may be converted into FDI in other areas of the world. In the same vein, China's contribution to raising the rate of return on FDI could twist investors' preference towards FDI instead of other private capital flows (mainly portfolio or cross-border lending), particularly if their returns were not closely correlated with those on FDI. Moreover, China itself – with its huge saving rate – is an important source of FDI; outward FDI from China has increased by 66 per cent per year since its accession to the WTO, although it remains very low compared with FDI from the largest OECD countries.

A third aspect to consider is the nature of Chinese inward FDI. If oriented towards exports, it might reduce FDI in other countries competing in the same export markets. This effect will be less strong if FDI is oriented towards China's domestic demand. In addition, if FDI substantially increases Chinese imports, it might foster FDI to other countries that supply Chinese imports, particularly exporters of commodities, which are scarce in China.

It thus seems clear that the impact of Chinese inward FDI on Latin American countries is an empirical question. Very few attempts to address this issue appear in the literature. A first step – even if only descriptive – is in IDB (2004). It depicts the evolution of cumulative bilateral FDI flows to Latin America and to China and calculates a coincidence index of FDI home countries, which appears to be low. Chantasasawat *et al.* (2004) analyse empirically whether China is taking FDI away from other Asian and Latin American countries. They find that the level of Chinese inward FDI is positively related to other Asian economies' inward FDI and that there is practically no impact on Latin American countries. Conducting the same exercise on the shares of FDI, they do show a negative Chinese effect on the Asian and Latin American shares.

This study goes beyond Chantasasawat *et al.* (2004) in a number of ways. *First*, it uses bilateral (homehost) and not aggregate data. Bilateral data much better describe investors' behaviour, avoid a potential aggregation bias and limit collinearity problems. *Second*, it not only estimates the impact of Chinese inward FDI on Latin America as a whole, but also differentiates among countries, because their productive structures and the types of FDI they attract differ greatly. For instance, Mexico and Central America have mainly received export-oriented FDI, while South America has attracted FDI mainly into the non-tradable sector (financial services and utilities) as well as natural-resource extraction. One would therefore expect China to have a negative impact on the first group, but not on the second, where it could even turn positive as China steps up its demand for commodities.

Third, Chantasasawat *et al.* (2004) assume the supply of FDI to be inelastic – a quite restrictive assumption for emerging countries, which have to compete for financing – while this study allows for the possibility of an elastic supply of FDI by introducing other capital flows as an additional factor. In this way, it captures potential substitution or complementarities among flows. *Fourth*, it takes into account the adjustment cost of FDI, which is known to be relevant for long-term (generally physical) investment, such as FDI. *Fifth*, it improves on the methodology to analyse the observed phenomena. It uses the generalised method of moments (GMM), instrumenting potentially endogenous variables with lags, exogenous variables and other valid instruments in order to obtain estimators unbiased, consistent and as efficient as possible. *Finally*, it compares different time spans to assess whether China's impact on other countries' inward FDI is a recent phenomenon, linked to the negotiations and final participation in the WTO, or already had begun after China announced it would open up its economy at the end of the 1970s.

Determinants of FDI

A wealth of empirical work has analysed the main determinants of inward FDI, with very little consensus except perhaps for the size of the host country's economy[3]. For a long time, the general view held that the "better" a country, in terms of its macroeconomic situation and institutional environment, the more easily it would attract FDI. For example, Albuquerque *et al.* (2002) find that macroeconomic stability increases FDI. Hines (1995) and Wei (1997) show that corruption discourages it, and the same is true for poor business operating conditions (Singh and Jun, 1995) or the inability to repatriate profits (Mody *et al.*, (1998). In the same vein, a survey of over 1 000 chief executives of multinational enterprises concludes that macroeconomic and political stability as well as the regulatory environment and country size are keys to foreign direct investors' decisions on where to establish themselves (AT Kearney, 2003).

Haussmann and Fernandez-Arias (2000), however, challenged this view, showing evidence that poor performers in terms of lower GDP per capita and less macroeconomic stability tend to attract more FDI. He also finds that countries with poorer institutions tend to attract more FDI as a share of total private capital flows. Another variable for which there is clearly no consensus is human capital. While it generally helps increase the marginal productivity of capital, this might not be so in lowskill, labour-intensive countries where low salaries mostly attract FDI (Chantasasawat *et al.*, 2003). As for the size of the economy, Jaumotte (2004) and Love and LageHidalgo (2000), among others, show evidence that the host country's total GDP and GDP per capita, respectively, help to attract more FDI. In addition, openness to trade also appears relevant (Singh and Jun, 1995; Albuquerque *et al.*, 2003).

Another strand of the literature has concentrated on the relation between trade and FDI (Brainard, 1997). Some studies find evidence of a substitution effect between the two while others argue in favour of complementarities. Substitution should in principle result when countries exporting a certain good decide to produce it in the destination country to avoid import or export tariffs. Complementarities could exist if FDI is export-oriented and requires importing inputs from the home country. Finally, some authors have concentrated on the role of push factors, either home-country or global, although there is no clear consensus on which ones are key. Albuquerque *et al.* (2002) report that push factors explain more than 50 per cent of FDI developments. In the same vein, LevyYeyati *et al.* (2002) show that the economic cycle in industrial countries is a relevant determinant of FDI, but the directions of influence change for the United States, Japan and Europe.

Variables and Data Issues

The dependent variable used here consists of annual bilateral inward FDI flows from the different OECD home countries to the six largest host economies of Latin America, expressed in millions of US dollars. The host countries are Argentina, Brazil, Chile, Colombia, Mexico and Venezuela (the full list of home and host countries is shown in Table 5-A1). The analysis is limited to these six because they are the only Latin American destinations included in the only database available on such flows for a large number of countries, namely the OECD's *International Direct Investment Statistics* (Table 4-A2 gives details on data sources).

There are two alternative time horizons. The longest possible one, given data availability, starts close to China's decision to conduct an open-door policy and runs from 1984 until 2001. This yields an unbalanced panel of 2 850 observations of bilateral FDI flows. Nonetheless, due to the missing values in the explanatory variables, this first model is estimated with a maximum of 527 observations[4]. Second, since the pattern of FDI flows appears to have changed since the mid-1990s, a shorter panel (1995-2001) is estimated. This period should also capture foreign investors' behaviour in the light of China's negotiations for WTO membership. This case permits only a maximum of 428 observations in the estimations.

The objective variable consists of bilateral inward FDI flows from different OECD countries to China. If there were a substitution effect from Latin American inward FDI towards China, the sign of its coefficient would be negative. The data are drawn from the same OECD source. This implies that they exclude important suppliers of FDI to China from the Asian region but outside the OECD. In reality, it is hard to think of potential competition between China and Latin America for FDI from Asian economies such as Hong Kong China, Macao China, Chinese Taipei or Singapore, which together accounted for 44 per cent of FDI in China in 2003. The cultural and ethnic ties between China and Asian nonOECD countries suggest a fragmentation in the FDI market. Including these countries as FDI providers could actually distort the answer to the question posed here, namely whether global foreign direct investors have reduced their FDI in Latin America because of China. FDI to Latin America originates mainly in OECD countries, which accounted for 76 per cent of the total received in 2002. The work thus focuses on FDI from them, to guarantee a relatively high degree of integration of the relevant FDI market and therefore real opportunities for substitution among destination countries.

Another objective variable, constructed as a robustness test, reflects bilateral inward FDI to Hong Kong China. Much reinvesting takes place between it and China, and it is not adequately accounted for in the statistics. This phenomenon, generally known as round-tripping, starts with China's exporting capital to Hong Kong China, favoured by tax advantages. This capital then returns to China in the form of FDI.

The other potentially relevant determinants of FDI, included as control variables, are classified into: *i)* capital flows, *ii)* bilateral variables, *iii)* host-country factors, *iv)* home-country variables and *v)* global factors. Adding them, the model estimated could be expressed as follows:

$$FDI_{i,t}^{j} = \lambda + \gamma \times FDI_{i,t-1}^{j} + \eta_1 \times FDI_{China,t}^{j} + \sum \alpha \times \text{capital flows}_t$$
$$+ \sum \beta \times \text{bilateral factors}_{i,t}^{j} + \sum \chi \times \text{host factors}_{i,t} + \sum \delta \times \text{home factors}_t^{j}$$
$$+ \sum \phi \times \text{global factors}_t + \varepsilon_{i,t}^{j}$$

I = host country (Latin America)
J = home country (OECD)

Capital flows include a number of factors. *First*, developments in other (portfolio and cross-border) capital flows are considered, to account for potential substitution between different types of investment. If it exists, the coefficient would have to be negative and significant. The data are drawn from the IMF *International Financial Statistics* (IFS). *Second*, one must allow for the possible persistence of FDI flows because investment requires time to adjust to desired levels. This is accounted for by taking the lag of the dependent variable. A *third* regressor considers the behaviour of other exporters of FDI, to determine whether investment decisions are influenced by what competitors do. Taking this into account involves including FDI from the whole OECD area to Latin America as well as to China and Hong Kong China. A positive and significant coefficient would indicate some kind of herd or "follow your competitor" behaviour among foreign direct investors. The *fourth* covers the possibility that FDI decisions may be taken at a regional level. In other words, if a country invests in, say, Chile, this could encourage additional investment in other Latin American countries. *Fifth*, FDI to OECD countries is introduced to test whether a possible preference of foreign direct investors to be present only in industrial countries discourages FDI to Latin America. *Finally*, the analysis controls for global trends in FDI flows, because it will certainly be easier for Latin American countries to receive investment during boom years for FDI. All these variables (except the first) are drawn from the OECD database.

Bilateral factors include the bilateral nominal exchange rate because it affects both the cost of the investment – if paid in local currency – and the value of repatriated profits. A depreciation of the host-country currency against the home-country one reduces both, so that the expected sign of the coefficient is not clear *a-priori*. The data are drawn from the IFS, and an increase implies a depreciation of the host currency against the home one. A measure of the relative investment cost is added, as measured by the difference in shortterm interest rates between the host and the home country, also from the IFS. The coefficient of this variable should in principle be negative but only if the investment is financed locally; otherwise it would be the home interest rate or an international one that matters. In addition, data on bilateral exports and imports from the IMF *Direction of Trade Statistics* (DOT) allow control for potential substitutability or complementarity between exports/imports and inward FDI. The final bilateral variable is an index of similarity in the home-country and host-country production structures, based on two-digit manufactured value-added data, from the United Nations Industrial Development Organization (UNIDO)[5]. This variable should indicate how similar the economies are and to what extent they may compete in third markets.

There are a number of potentially relevant host factors. Macroeconomic conditions related to the external sector, such as the level of external debt to GDP, the debt service, international reserves and export growth are included. Although no strong consensus exists on their influence, the first two should in principle bear a negative relation with inward FDI while the last two, particularly export growth, should be positively related. Other host macroeconomic conditions are GDP growth, the ratio of domestic investment to GDP and the fiscal balance, whose coefficients should in principle be positive. Inflation and the real exchange rate may be expected to reduce inward FDI insofar as they lower the host country's competitiveness. All these variables come from the IFS and the World Bank's World Development Indicators (WDI). Finally, the size of the economy should in principle foster FDI. It is proxied by a combination of GDP per capita and GDP[6], both in dollars. The two are drawn from the WDI and the IMF World Economic Outlook (WEO) database, respectively. Countries' endowments of natural resources are drawn from Haussmann and Fernandez-Arias (2000). Finally, due to the restrictions imposed by the methodology used – only time-variant variables can be considered – only a few host-country institutional characteristics are included, namely capital-account restrictions, drawn from Lane and Milesi-Ferretti (2004), the quality of creditor rights from the International Country Risk Guide database, and human capital, proxied by the literacy level from the WDI database. The first should discourage capital flows, including FDI, and the last two should yield a positive effect. As with the macroeconomic variables, however, one should not forget the general lack of strong consensus on their effects. Finally, for financial crises one dummy variable is included for each type of crisis – sovereign, currency or banking – which takes the value of one in each year in which a country finds itself in crisis. This allows capture of the cumulative impact of each of these events[7]. The information is drawn from Díaz-Cassou *et al.* (2006). Crises generally should discourage foreign investors, but banking crises tend to be followed by the opening of the banking system to foreign competition, mainly through privatisation. This could attract FDI.

For home-county effects GDP growth and GDP per capita from the WEO database are included. Developments in oil prices are taken as the main global factor affecting FDI. They are drawn from DataStream. Table 5-A3 shows the bilateral correlations between all these regressors.

Empirical Methodology

In undertaking the empirical analysis, a number of methodological issues need to be addressed such as endogeneity, how to capture adjustment costs of FDI, unobserved heterogeneity and the choice of the control variables. To tackle potential endogeneity as well as the existence of adjustment costs and unobserved heterogeneity, the analysis uses the GMM, following Arellano and Bover (1995). The Arellano-Bover estimator – also called the system GMM estimator – combines the regression expressed in first differences (lagged values of the variables in levels are used as instruments) with the original equation expressed in levels (this equation is instrumented with lagged differences of the variables) and allows inclusion of some additional instruments.

This option is preferred to a fixed-effects estimator for several reasons. *First*, it takes into account unobserved time-invariant bilateral specific effects. *Second*, one can tackle the potential endogeneity arising from the inclusion of the lagged dependent variable (to capture the adjustment costs) and other potentially endogenous variables in the righthand side of the equation, such as bilateral FDI to Latin America, other FDI flows and bilateral trade[8]. *Third*, it deals with the possibility that the dependent variable is not stationary. *Finally*, considering all possible instruments it achieves a high degree of efficiency.

The GMM estimators have two main disadvantages, however. First, because their properties hold asymptotically, it would be safer to use this methodology with a very large number of observations[9]. As a robustness test, all regressions are run as a fixed-effect panel with robust standard errors. The results do not differ too much. The other disadvantage is that one cannot include time-invariant regressors because their coefficients are not identifiable with this methodology. This does not imply that there is a problem of omitted variables, however, because they are all included in the time-invariant country-specific effects.

To tackle omitted variables, first a general equation including all control variables considered is estimated (column one of Tables 5.1 and 5.2); then, a Wald test evaluates the joint hypothesis that the coefficients of the variables that are not significant individually are equal to zero. If it is not rejected, the model is re-estimated with only the significant controls. Otherwise, a less restrictive hypothesis is tested, still trying to reduce the number of regressors to the maximum extent possible. This sequential – from general to specific[10] – strategy is followed until one can reject that the remaining set of coefficients of the control variables is equal to zero (column two of Tables 5.1 and 5.2). This procedure achieves more efficient coefficients on the remaining parameters, including that of the variable of interest, i.e. Chinese inward FDI. The last model, apart from incorporating these restrictions on the regressors included, tests whether the effect of Chinese inward FDI is different across the Latin American countries (column three of Tables 5.1 and 5.2).

Results

The analysis, as described, regresses the six largest Latin American countries' inward FDI on bilateral FDI to China and controls for the all aforementioned regressors in the unrestricted model. The first step uses the whole sample from 1984 to 2001. This captures developments shortly after China started its open door policy until the most recent data coinciding with China's entry into the WTO. When all controls are introduced, no evidence emerges of a substitution effect from Latin American FDI to China (Table 5.1, column one). The same is true for FDI to Hong Kong China. Then, with the number of control variables reduced, the lack of a significant impact of Chinese inward FDI is confirmed (Table 5.1, column two).

Regarding the impact of China on the inward FDI of each of the Latin American countries considered, Argentina and Colombia are negatively affected at the 5 per cent and 10 per cent significance levels, respectively, but the parameters are very small (Table 5.1, column three). In addition, one cannot

Table 5.1. Results for the Long Time Span: 1984-2001

Dependent variable: Bilateral FDI flow from home to host countries	(1) Common Effect for all Latin American Countries Coefficient	P-Value	(2) (1) + Jointly Non-Significant Coefficients Removed Coefficient	P-Value	(3) (2) + Individual Effect for Each Latin American Country (a) Coefficient	P-Value
Latin America as a whole						
Bilateral FDI to China	-0.068	(0.234)	-0.062	(0.245)		
Bilateral FDI to HK, China	-0.033	(0.574)				
Country-specific (b): Impact of FDI to China on FDI:						
To Argentina					-0.095**	(0.043)
To Brazil					0.131	(0.383)
To Chile					0.075	(0.489)
To Colombia					0.228*	(0.091)
To Mexico					-0.068	(0.295)
To Venezuela					-0.062	(0.487)
Control Variables						
Capital flows						
Total capital flows over GDP	-16.535	(0.163)	9.357***	(0.002)	8.775***	(0.002)
Lag of bilateral FDI	0.259	(0.258)	0.221	(0.172)	0.312	(0.140)
OECD FDI to China	0.003	(0.329)				
OECD FDI to HK, China	0.006	(0.398)				
OECD FDI to Latin America	-0.001	(0.308)				
Total FDI of OECD Members	0.000	(0.448)				
Bilateral FDI to Latin America	0.061***	(0.002)	0.060***	(0.004)	0.051***	(0.003)
Bilateral FDI to OECD	0.002	(0.156)	0.001	(0.149)	0.001	(0.118)
Bilateral Variables						
Bilat. nominal exchange rate (c)	0.398**	(0.018)	0.082	(0.134)	0.099*	(0.067)
Host-home int. rate differential	0.164	(0.414)				
Exports	0.074**	(0.012)	0.038***	(0.007)	0.037***	(0.007)
Imports	-0.029	(0.409)				
Similarity in prod. structure	36.881	(0.808)	94.095	(0.258)	91.405	(0.256)
Host-country variables						
Macro variables						
External debt to GDP	-4.335	(0.571)				
Debt service to GDP	-95.210**	(0.018)				
External reserves	-0.012	(0.280)				
Export growth	-1.772	(0.620)				
GDP growth	40.084**	(0.024)	7.707	(0.162)	6.507	(0.205)
Inflation	-0.592	(0.225)				
Fiscal balance	-17.023	(0.384)				
Domestic investment/GDP	-18.733	(0.199)				
Real effective exchg. rate (d)	-0.831	(0.495)				

Table 5.1 continued

	(1) Common Effect for all Latin American Countries		(2) (1) + Jointly Non-Significant Coefficients Removed		(3) (2) + Individual Effect for Each Latin American Country (a)	
Dependent variable: Bilateral FDI flow from home to host countries	Coefficient	P-Value	Coefficient	P-Value	Coefficient	P-Value
General characteristics						
Size	0.000	(0.540)				
Natural resources	1.045**	(0.043)	0.221**	(0.049)	0.216*	(0.055)
Institutional characteristics						
Capital account restrictions	166.729	(0.372)				
Creditor rights	32.538	(0.583)				
Literacy	81.430	(0.243)	15.644	(0.150)	13.752	(0.149)
Occurrence of crises						
Sovereign	-94.170	(0.448)				
Banking	459.129***	(0.007)	147.731***	(0.009)	135.266**	(0.010)
Currency	-157.281	(0.232)				
Home-country variables						
GDP growth	-31.985	(0.138)	-4.837	(0.219)	-3.288	(0.334)
GDP per capita	0.000	(0.957)				
Global Shocks: Oil price	6.699	(0.701)				
Constant	-7153.329	(0.246)	-1707.054	(0.114)	-1520.144	(0.112)
F-statistic	42678.81	(0.000)	497.36	(0.000)	1430.84	(0.000)
Observations	339		527		527	
Number of groups (home, host)	65		87		87	

Notes: Robust P-values are in parentheses. * = significant at 10%. ** = significant at 5%. *** = significant at 1%. Variables in italics are instrumented through the GMM procedure following Arellano and Bover (1995). Variables removed in columns (2) and (3) are jointly not significant at a 95 per cent confidence interval. The categorical variables *rating* and *civil and political liberties* are also included as regressors. (a) Although control variables' coefficients differ numerically from column (2), the results are qualitatively the same. (b) These variables result from multiplying FDI to China and a dummy variable that takes the value of one for the observations of each of the host countries. (c) Increase indicates depreciation of host currency. (d) Increase indicates an appreciation of the real effective exchange rate.

reject the hypothesis that the coefficients of each Latin American country are the same and equal to zero. Given the weakness of these two results, one can generally conclude that there is virtually no "Chinese effect" on Latin American inward FDI in this long time span.

To report on the significance of the control variables, we focus on the restricted model because the estimators are more efficient[11]. First, there is a strong and significant complementarity effect between FDI and other private capital flows, as the coefficient for total capital flows over GDP is positive and highly significant. This result supports the hypothesis of an elastic supply of FDI. Second, there is a certain degree of a "regional" effect, because an increase in FDI to a given Latin American country from a given home country raises investment in other countries of the region. This is shown in the highly significant, albeit small, coefficient on bilateral FDI to Latin America. Third, the amount of bilateral exports also appears to foster FDI, which supports the hypothesis of complementarity – not substitution – between the two. One possible interpretation is that FDI received by Latin American countries is export-oriented, at least in certain countries, and therefore fosters exports. Fourth, as one would expect, the availability of natural resources in the host countries contributes to higher inward FDI. Finally and interestingly, the occurrence of banking crises appears to foster FDI in all three specifications. The causal link probably lies less in the banking crises themselves than in the privatisation and opening to foreign competition that have followed them in practically all Latin American countries in the sample[12]. Finally, the fixed effects estimated for each home-host pair also pick up the information of the regressors, which barely change over time. This could explain why they are not found significant.

The second exercise restricts the panel to a more recent time span, from 1995 to 2001, for a number of reasons. First, there may have been a structural change in the evolution of FDI since the mid-1990s. Second, China accelerated its negotiations for WTO membership in this period, before it finally acceded in 2001. An additional, more technical, reason is that the potential problem of non-stationarity (although considered in the Arellano-Bover methodology) is clearly reduced for this shorter time span.

In this period, a clearly negative and significant effect of Chinese inward FDI on that to Latin America emerges (Table 5.2, columns one and two). In a country-by-country analysis of the impact, Mexico and Colombia are negatively and significantly affected by increases in Chinese inward FDI — particularly Mexico, at a 99 per cent confidence level (95 per cent for Colombia).

Table 5.2. **Results for the Shorter Time Span: 1995-2001**

Dependent variable: Bilateral FDI flow from home to host countries	(1) Common Effect for all Latin American Countries Coefficient	P-Value	(2) (1) + Jointly Non-Significant Coefficients Removed Coefficient	P-Value	(3) (2) + Individual Effect for Each Latin American Country (a) Coefficient	P-Value
Objective Variables						
Latin America as a whole						
Bilateral FDI to China	-0.154*	(0.065)	-0.157**	(0.024)		
Bilateral FDI to HK, China	-0.084	(0.299)				
Country-specific (b): Impact of FDI to China on FDI:						
To Argentina					-0.083	(0.244)
To Brazil					-0.219	(0.260)
To Chile					0.035	(0.737)
To Colombia					-0.844**	(0.013)
To Mexico					-0.287***	(0.007)
To Venezuela					-0.204	(0.230)
Control Variables						
Capital flows						
Total capital flows over GDP	42.349**	(0.034)	9.168	(0.193)	7.464	(0.296)
Lag of bilateral FDI	0.031	(0.877)	0.046	(0.259)	0.064*	(0.055)
OECD FDI to China	-0.002	(0.430)				
OECD FDI to HK, China	0.023**	(0.018)				
OECD FDI to Latin America	-0.004*	(0.013)				
Total FDI of OECD Members	0.000	(0.379)				
Bilateral FDI to Latin America	0.086**	(0.004)	0.121***	(0.001)	0.108***	(0.001)
Bilateral FDI to OECD	0.001	(0.177)				
Bilateral Variables						
Bilat. nominal exchange rate (c)	0.621**	(0.020)	0.179**	(0.045)	0.276***	(0.008)
Host-home int. rate differential	-3.149	(0.158)				
Exports	0.203***	(0.001)	0.247***	(0.000)	0.250***	(0.002)
Imports	-0.121**	(0.033)	-0.168***	(0.003)	-0.167**	(0.011)
Similarity in prod. structure	97.138	(0.682)				
Host-country variables						
Macro variables						
External debt to GDP	-3.307	(0.667)				
Debt service to GDP	122.735**	(0.043)				
External reserves	-0.019	(0.130)	-0.007	(0.151)	-0.005	(0.250)
Export growth	5.459	(0.374)				
GDP growth	-33.646	(0.260)				
Inflation	8.161	(0.165)				
Fiscal balance	-94.879	(0.170)				
Domestic investment/GDP	29.968	(0.507)				
Real effective exchg. rate (d)	-1.911	(0.530)				

Table 5.2. (continued)

Dependent variable: Bilateral FDI flow from home to host countries	(1) Common Effect for all Latin American Countries Coefficient	P-Value	(2) (1) + Jointly Non-Significant Coefficients Removed Coefficient	P-Value	(3) (2) + Individual Effect for Each Latin American Country (a) Coefficient	P-Value
General characteristics						
Size	0.000	(0.450)				
Natural resources	1.702**	(0.044)	0.677**	(0.022)	0.621**	(0.032)
Institutional characteristics						
Creditor rights	47.222	(0.410)				
Literacy	193.501**	(0.026)	46.056*	(0.085)	35.217	(0.189)
Occurrence of crises						
Sovereign	-195.527	(0.347)				
Banking	-398.843	(0.128)	222.233***	(0.000)	217.170***	(0.001)
Currency	53.805	(0.773)				
Home-country variables						
GDP growth	-7.787	(0.702)				
GDP per capita	0.007	(0.260)				
Constant	-20930.168	(0.026)	-4928.704	(0.062)	-3882.54	(0.138)
F-statistic	6425.51	(0.000)	338.92	(0.000)	291.51	(0.000)
Observations	172		428		428	
Number of groups (home, host)	60		99		99	

Notes: Robust P-values are in parentheses. * = significant at 10%. ** = significant at 5%. *** = significant at 1%. Variables in italics are instrumented through the GMM procedure following Arellano and Bover (1995). Variables removed in columns (2) and (3) are jointly not significant at a 95% confidence interval. (a) Although control variables' coefficients differ numerically with column (2), the results are qualitatively the same. (b) These variables result from multiplying FDI to China and a dummy variable that takes the value of one for the observations of each of the host countries. (c) An increase indicates depreciation of the host-country currency. (d) An increase indicates appreciation of the real effective exchange rate.

As Table 5.2 shows, when Chinese inward FDI increases by $100 million, Colombian and Mexican inward FDI flows are reduced by $84 million and $29 million respectively. Notwithstanding the relatively large difference in the parameters, the impact could be similar since one cannot reject the hypothesis that both coefficients are statistically equal. This result is particularly interesting for Mexico because the North American Free Trade Agreement (NAFTA) was in place during the whole period and inward FDI generally increased. In fact, it began to fall only more recently, in 2002, but this does not imply that China had no effect. The results should be read in terms of a counterfactual: had Chinese inward FDI not been so strong, Mexico could have attracted more FDI than it actually did. Finally, excluding the impact on Mexico and Colombia, no dislocation can be found from the other Latin America countries to China[13].

Results for control variables are very similar to those for the longer panel, except for two. The bilateral nominal exchange depreciation is now clearly significant in increasing FDI to Latin American countries, which hints that lower investment cost, because of the exchange-rate depreciation, weighs more than a reduction in repatriated benefits. In addition, larger bilateral imports seem to imply less Latin American inward FDI. This result is in line with the hypothesis of substitution between imports and FDI and hints at the existence of a large share of FDI geared towards domestic demand for Latin American countries as a group. Considering this result together with the previous on export complementarity, it could well be that the complementarity stems from countries with more export-oriented FDI, such as Mexico, and the substitutability of imports comes from some of the South American countries. In any event, this hypothesis cannot be tested because the data contain only Latin American aggregate coefficients for the control variables.

Finally, a number of robustness tests do not change the results[14]. The first one tackles the close relation between Hong Kong China's and Chinese inward FDI, taking as the objective variable the sum of FDI to China and Hong Kong China. Second, the extreme hypothesis of complete substitution from Latin American inward FDI to that of China is tested. As could be expected from the results, the hypothesis is rejected. Third, the regressions are run taking logs for all variables for which this is possible. Fourth, the potential endogeneity of the bilateral exchange rate is accounted for by taking instruments. The fifth test controls for the potential endogeneity of the externality associated with total FDI to Latin America excluding the FDI of the host country.

Conclusions

This chapter investigates how Chinese inward FDI affects FDI flows to Latin American countries. Over the long period from 1984 to 2001 it finds hardly any evidence of FDI dislocation from Latin American countries to China, but such dislocation does seem to be present in a more recent period (1995-2001) that focuses on the years when FDI flows grew more rapidly worldwide and negotiations for China's WTO membership accelerated. This arises from a significant negative impact on Mexican and Colombian inward FDI, while the other Latin American countries are not affected. Given that FDI generally increased during the period, these results probably imply that: had Chinese inward FDI not been so strong, these two countries could have attracted more FDI.

This suggests that competing in the same sectors as China increases the likelihood of an FDI substitution. A cursory look at the sectoral structure of FDI in Mexico and Colombia shows that manufacturing accounts for 56 per cent of the total in Mexico (the largest of all sectors) and 21 per cent (the largest after financial services) in Colombia. By contrast, Brazil has a much smaller share of FDI in manufacturing (about 10 per cent) while most of it concentrates on telecommunications and financial services[15]. In any event, this interpretation is only tentative because not enough evidence exists that this is the main channel through which China affects Latin American FDI. In fact, because the focus of the chapter is on the behaviour of global investors, the authors opted for bilateral rather than sectoral data so that not much can be said about the channels by which China may influence other host countries. Both bilateral and sectoral data would be ideal but they are not available.

Looking into the future there are reasons to expect that China will continue to receive large amounts of FDI and perhaps even increase them. The country is bound to embark on a large privatisation process, which has already been announced for some sectors. In addition, the wage differential with Latin American countries will probably continue for quite some time given China's large – for some close to infinite – elasticity of labour supply. Finally, even if wages increase substantially, they will boost the purchasing power of a very large population. This will make China a particularly attractive country for FDI targeting domestic demand.

The scenario in which China continues to attract a large share of world FDI may seem worrisome for Latin American countries, particularly those with productive structures more similar to China's. This reflects only one side of the coin, however. Heavy FDI in China also provides tremendous opportunities in the medium term. For geographical reasons, Latin American countries are not as well positioned as Asian economies to reap some of these benefits, such as assembling and re-exporting manufactured products – yet they will clearly benefit from China's increasing demand for raw materials in a scenario where it continues to grow fast. This applies not only to Latin American exports, but also to inward FDI in sectors related to raw materials. Interestingly, potential investors in the region are not only the global players included in our database, basically OECD countries, but also China itself, which will want to ensure its access to raw materials. The further opening of these sectors to foreign investors is a pre-condition for Latin American countries to reap these benefits of China's increasing global presence.

Notes

1. Both authors were affiliated with Banco de España at the time of writing. Alicia Garcia-Herrero is now working as an economist at the Hong Kong branch of the Bank of International Settlements (BIS). The opinions expressed are theirs and not necessarily those of Banco de España. They would like to thank Juan Carlos Berganza, Luis Molina, José Manuel Montero and Juan Ruiz for their clarifications on data and methodological issues. They are also grateful for suggestions from participants in the First LAEBA Conference on the Challenges and Opportunities of the Emergence of China and in a Banco de España seminar, as well as Javier Vallés and an anonymous referee. Remaining errors are obviously their own.

2. These figures are drawn from IMF *International Financial Statistics*.

3. Reviewing the reasons behind the lack of consensus is beyond the scope of this paper, but two very important ones are the lack of reliable data (Singh and Jun, 1995) and the difference between horizontal and vertical FDI (Ewe Ghee, 2001).

4. This is the number of observations in the restricted model (after eliminating jointly non-significant parameters). In the general model the number of observations is lower, 339, because of missing values in the non-significant regressors.

5. The construction of this measure of economic similarity follows García-Herrero and Ruiz (2004). It is expressed as

$$S_{j,i,t} = -\sum_{n=1}^{N} |s_{n,j,t} - s_{n,i,t}|$$

    where N is the number of sectors. Note that $S_{i,j,t}$ represents the average of discrepancies in economic structures in the period t. $S_{i,j,t}$ might take values between 0 for identical structures and -2 for disjoint productive structures. Therefore higher values for $S_{i,j,t}$ imply more similarity between the host and home productive structures.

6. Both variables are also controlled for separately and the results do not change.

7. To test the robustness of the results a different dummy takes the value of one only in the first year of the crisis.

8. A robustness test also instruments for the bilateral nominal exchange rate. The results do not change.

9. In any event, the small-sample problem is less acute for the Arellano-Bover estimator than the Arellano-Bond one, because it has been shown to provide more accurate estimations in small samples (Bond, 2002). Additionally, this estimator does not require time stationarity as long as T is small, which seems to be the case here.

10. See Campos *et al.* (2005) for details on the general-to-specific strategy.

11. The bilateral nominal exchange rate, the debt service and GDP growth in the host country are significant only in the first specification with all regressors. The nonsignificance in the restricted model may be due to the increased number of observations and degrees of freedom.

12. That this result is found only for the dummy that considers all crisis years and not only the burst of the crisis supports this interpretation.

13. In other words one cannot reject that the coefficients of Argentina, Brazil, Chile and Venezuela are the same and equal to zero.

14. The results of these tests are available on request.

15. This has been estimated using FDI flows from the three main investors in Brazil, namely the United States, Spain and Japan. Unfortunately, one cannot compare Mexico and Colombia with the other Latin American countries included in the analysis because the authors could not find sectoral information.

Table 5-A-1. **List of Countries Considered**

Home Country	Host Country	Additional Countries or Areas
Australia	Argentina	China
Austria	Brazil	Hong Kong, China
Belgium	Chile	Latin America
Canada	Colombia	OECD
Czech Republic	Mexico	World
Denmark	Venezuela	
Finland		
France		
Germany		
Greece		
Hungary		
Iceland		
Ireland		
Italy		
Japan		
Korea		
Mexico		
Netherlands		
New Zealand		
Norway		
Poland		
Portugal		
Slovak Republic		
Spain		
Sweden		
Switzerland		
Turkey		
United Kingdom		

Table 5-A-2. **Variables and Data Sources**

Variable Type	Name	Description	Units	Source
Bilateral	Bilateral FDI	Bilateral FDI	$ millions	OECD
Bilateral	Bilateral exchange rate	Bilateral exchange rate; increase implies depreciation in home currency	Host per home currency	IFS, IMF
Bilateral	Bilateral exports	Bilateral export flows	$ millions	DOT, IMF
Bilateral	Bilateral imports	Bilateral import flows	$ millions	DOT, IMF
Bilateral	Host-home interest rate differential	Host-home differential in short-term interest rates	Percentage	IFS, IMF
Bilateral	Similarity in production structures	Index of similarity in production structures	Index	UNIDO
Capital flows	Bilateral FDI to China	Level of FDI flows of each home country to China	$ millions	OECD
Capital flows	Bilateral FDI to Hong Kong, China	Level of FDI flows of each home country to Hong Kong, China	$ millions	OECD
Capital flows	Bilateral FDI to Latin America	Level of FDI flows of each home country to the six Latin American countries included	$ millions	OECD
Capital flows	Bilateral FDI to OECD	Level of FDI flows of each home country in the OECD	$ millions	OECD
Capital flows	OECD FDI into OECD	FDI of all OECD countries in OECD area	$ millions	OECD
Capital flows	OECD FDI to China	Level of FDI of all OECD Members to China	$ millions	OECD
Capital flows	OECD FDI to Hong Kong, China	Level of FDI of all OECD Members to Hong Kong, China	$ millions	OECD
Capital flows	OECD FDI to Latin America	Level of FDI of all OECD Members to Latin America	$ millions	OECD
Capital flows	Total FDI of OECD Members	FDI of all OECD Members to the world	$ millions	OECD
Global	Oil Price	Brent crude	$/bbl, monthly	Datastream
Home	GDP Growth in Home Country	Growth rate of GDP at constant prices	Percentage	WEO, IMF
Home	GDP per Capita, Home Country	GDP per capita at current prices	Dollars	WEO, IMF

Host	Capital Account Restrictions	Dummy: = 1 if the country had capital-account restrictions; = 0 otherwise		Miles-Ferrati (1998)
Host	Creditor Rights	Contract viability, profits repatriation, payment delays		PRS Group
Host	Debt Service to GDP	Interest expenditures plus amortisation	Per cent of GDP	World Bank
Host	Domestic Investment over GDP	Fixed capital investment	Per cent of GDP	World Bank
Host	Export Growth	Annual growth of exports valued in dollars	Per cent	World Bank
Host	External Debt to GDP	Total external debt	Per cent of GDP	World Bank
Host	External Reserves	Total reserves minus gold	$ millions	IFS, IMF
Host	Fiscal Balance	Public-sector balance (positive indicates surplus; negative indicates deficit)	Per cent of GDP	IFS, IMF
Host	GDP Growth	Real annual GDP growth rate	Per cent	IFS, IMF
Host	Inflation	CPI annual growth rate	Per cent	IFS, IMF
Host	Literacy	Adult (over 15) literacy rate	Per cent	World Bank
Host	Natural Resources	Natural resources valuation	$ millions (PPP)	Haussmann (2001)
Host	Occurrence of Banking Crises	Dummy: = 1 if banking crisis in a given year		Diaz et al. (2004)
Host	Occurrence of Exchange Crises	Dummy: = 1 if currency crisis in a given year		Diaz et al. (2004)
Host	Occurrence of Sovereign Crises	Dummy: = 1 if country in default in a given year		Diaz et al. (2004)
Host	Other Capital Flows over GDP	Portfolio and other investment flows	Per cent of GDP	IFS, IMF
Host	Political and Social Liberties	Political and social freedom: 0 = more freedom	Categorical	Freedom House
Host	Rating	Sovereign debt risk rating	Categorical	Moody's
Host	Real Effective Exchange Rate	Real effective exchange rates (an increase indicates an appreciation)	Index	IFS, IMF
Host	Short-term Interest Rate		Per cent	IFS, IMF
Host	Size	Product of GDP per capita and GDP		WEO, IMF

Table 5-A-3. Correlation Among Variables

	1	2	3	4	5	6	7	8	9	10	11
1. Bilateral FDI to China	1.00										
2. Bilateral FDI to Hong Kong, China	0.44	1.00									
3. Bilateral FDI to Latin America	0.34	0.55	1.00								
4. Bilateral FDI to OECD	0.29	0.55	0.36	1.00							
5. Bilateral exports	0.17	0.33	0.35	0.16	1.00						
6. Bilateral imports	0.15	0.32	0.32	0.15	0.99	1.00					
7. OECD FDI to China	0.23	0.06	0.13	0.19	0.05	0.04	1.00				
8. OECD FDI to Hong Kong, China	0.11	0.11	0.18	0.30	0.07	0.05	0.75	1.00			
9. OECD FDI to Latin America	0.09	0.09	0.22	0.35	0.07	0.06	0.71	0.90	1.00		
10. Total FDI of OECD countries	0.03	0.07	0.19	0.39	0.06	0.06	0.52	0.75	0.89	1.00	
11. External debt to GDP	-0.06	-0.04	-0.06	-0.09	0.06	-0.05	-0.28	-0.25	-0.21	-0.20	1.00
12. External reserves	0.08	0.04	0.12	0.19	0.12	0.10	0.59	0.60	0.61	0.52	-0.35
13. Export growth	0.04	0.02	-0.01	0.04	0.01	0.01	0.08	0.06	-0.01	0.06	-0.08
14. GDP Growth	0.02	0.01	-0.01	-0.03	0.00	0.00	0.09	0.12	0.03	-0.05	-0.13
15. Size	0.06	0.04	0.10	0.18	0.15	0.12	0.48	0.54	0.55	0.48	-0.42
16. Inflation	-0.04	0.00	-0.03	-0.05	-0.02	-0.01	-0.14	-0.03	-0.08	-0.11	-0.05
17. Fiscal balance	0.02	0.00	0.00	0.00	-0.02	-0.01	0.11	0.08	0.03	0.01	0.06
18. Debt service to GDP	-0.02	-0.01	0.01	0.03	0.01	0.01	-0.09	-0.08	0.00	0.07	0.69
19. Natural resources	0.00	0.00	0.00	0.00	0.06	0.07	0.00	0.00	0.00	0.00	-0.25
20. Capital account restrictions	0.00	0.01	0.03	0.05	0.01	0.02	0.06	0.13	0.17	0.13	0.09
21. Total capital flows over GDP	0.06	0.03	0.07	0.10	0.02	0.00	0.35	0.32	0.32	0.26	-0.50
22. Domestic investment over GDP	0.05	0.03	0.00	-0.02	0.05	0.04	0.08	0.05	-0.02	-0.07	-0.34
23. Sovereign crises	-0.07	-0.04	-0.08	-0.15	-0.05	-0.03	-0.36	-0.32	-0.32	-0.35	-0.40
24. Banking crises	0.03	-0.01	-0.03	-0.05	-0.02	0.02	0.01	-0.16	-0.15	-0.13	-0.19
25. Currency crises	-0.01	-0.01	0.01	0.01	-0.02	-0.02	-0.06	-0.11	0.04	0.03	0.29
26. Creditor rights	0.01	0.02	0.04	0.05	0.08	0.07	0.19	0.32	0.28	0.17	-0.33
27. Similarity in productive structures	-0.09	-0.13	-0.07	-0.13	0.03	0.02	-0.03	-0.05	-0.11	-0.12	-0.24
28. GDP growth in home country	-0.06	0.05	0.08	0.04	0.00	0.01	0.15	0.14	0.17	0.16	0.06
29. GDP per capita in home country	0.41	0.28	0.20	0.31	0.15	0.13	0.38	0.44	0.42	0.34	-0.13
30. Real effective exchange rate	-0.13	-0.24	-0.17	-0.18	-0.06	-0.06	-0.15	-0.18	-0.18	-0.16	0.04
31. Bilateral exchange rate	-0.01	0.07	0.13	0.26	-0.03	-0.03	0.22	0.27	0.29	0.28	-0.07
32. Host-home interest rate differential	-0.03	0.01	-0.02	-0.03	-0.01	0.00	-0.13	-0.03	-0.09	-0.08	0.02
33. Oil price	-0.05	-0.02	-0.01	0.07	0.01	0.02	-0.21	-0.25	-0.17	0.12	0.01
34. Literacy	0.05	0.03	0.08	0.13	-0.03	-0.04	0.34	0.41	0.42	0.35	0.15

Does China Have an Impact on Foreign Direct Investment to Latin America?

	12	13	14	15	16	17	18	19	20	21	22
12. External reserves	1.00										
13. Export growth	-0.01	1.00									
14. GDP Growth	0.06	0.10	1.00								
15. Size	0.89	0.02	0.02	1.00							
16. Inflation	-0.01	0.00	-0.17	0.07	1.00						
17. Fiscal balance	-0.07	0.10	0.18	-0.18	-0.21	1.00					
18. Debt service to GDP	-0.12	-0.08	-0.09	-0.20	-0.32	0.11	1.00				
19. Natural resources	0.46	0.02	-0.05	0.52	0.29	-0.53	-0.22	1.00			
20. Capital account restrictions	0.06	-0.18	0.04	0.02	0.09	-0.06	0.08	0.08	1.00		
21. Total capital flows over GDP	0.27	-0.04	0.29	0.16	-0.34	0.29	-0.22	-0.20	-0.16	1.00	
22. Domestic investment over GDP	0.06	0.10	0.40	0.07	-0.11	0.06	-0.16	0.04	-0.15	0.40	1.00
23. Sovereign crises	-0.30	-0.12	-0.04	-0.20	0.36	-0.30	0.04	0.20	0.12	-0.56	-0.21
24. Banking crises	0.11	-0.10	-0.21	0.11	0.16	-0.04	0.19	0.01	-0.08	-0.20	-0.14
25. Currency crises	-0.21	-0.02	-0.32	-0.11	0.08	-0.21	0.18	-0.06	0.09	-0.35	-0.25
26. Creditor rights	0.31	0.04	0.30	0.30	-0.18	0.34	-0.06	-0.10	-0.13	0.43	0.42
27. Similarity in productive structures	0.22	0.07	0.02	0.39	0.17	-0.21	-0.24	0.37	-0.12	-0.01	0.12
28. GDP growth in home country	0.07	0.10	0.01	0.07	0.00	-0.07	0.07	0.00	0.08	-0.05	-0.01
29. GDP per capita in home country	0.29	0.05	0.07	0.25	0.00	0.08	-0.06	0.00	0.07	0.15	0.02
30. Real effective exchange rate	-0.12	0.01	-0.01	-0.11	0.02	-0.01	0.01	0.00	-0.03	-0.07	0.01
31. Bilateral exchange rate	-0.11	-0.02	0.04	-0.23	-0.13	0.06	0.02	-0.33	0.09	0.15	-0.05
32. Host-home interest rate differential	-0.04	-0.05	-0.17	0.04	0.86	-0.15	-0.24	0.20	0.05	-0.30	-0.07
33. Oil price	-0.10	-0.05	-0.23	-0.07	-0.01	0.01	0.18	0.00	-0.04	-0.02	-0.28
34. Literacy	0.00	-0.05	0.03	-0.01	-0.10	0.46	0.07	-0.72	0.04	0.17	-0.10

	23	24	25	26	27	28	29	30	31	32	33
23. Sovereign crises	1.00										
24. Banking crises	-0.05	1.00									
25. Currency crises	0.19	0.30	1.00								
26. Creditor rights	-0.35	-0.22	-0.29	1.00							
27. Similarity in productive structures	0.02	0.00	-0.09	0.08	1.00						
28. GDP growth in home country	0.04	0.02	0.05	-0.10	-0.01	1.00					
29. GDP per capita in home country	-0.16	-0.09	0.00	0.15	-0.33	0.00	1.00				
30. Real effective exchange rate	0.06	0.02	0.00	-0.06	0.13	-0.01	-0.28	1.00			
31. Bilateral exchange rate	-0.22	-0.19	0.06	-0.03	-0.21	0.02	0.18	-0.03	1.00		
32. Host-home interest rate differential	0.26	0.20	-0.04	-0.16	0.11	0.02	0.01	0.02	-0.09	1.00	
33. Oil price	0.04	0.21	-0.03	0.06	-0.03	-0.04	-0.15	0.03	-0.02	-0.03	1.00
34. Literacy	-0.10	-0.01	0.06	0.22	-0.22	0.06	0.21	-0.09	0.17	-0.10	-0.10

Bibliography

ALBUQUERQUE, R., N. LOAYZA AND L. SERVÉN (2003), "World Market Integration through the Lens of Foreign Direct Investors", Policy Research Working Paper Series 3060, The World Bank, Washington, D.C.

ARELLANO, M. AND O. BOVER (1995), "Another Look at the Instrumental-Variable Estimation of Error-Components Models", *Journal of Econometrics*, Vol. 68, pp. 29-52.

KEARNEY, A.T. (2003), *FDI Confidence Index Reports, 19972002*. Available at: http://www.atkearney.com

BLUNDELL, R. AND S. BOND (1998), "Initial Conditions and Moment Restrictions in Dynamic Panel Data Models", *Journal of Econometrics*, 87, pp. 115-143.

BOND, S. (2002), "Dynamic Panel Data Models: A Guide to Micro Data Methods and Practice", Working Paper 09/02, Institute for Fiscal Studies, London.

BRAINARD, L. (1997). "An Empirical Assessment of the Proximity-Concentration Trade-off between Multinational Sales and Trade", *American Economic Review*, 87 (4), pp. 520-544.

CAMPOS, J., N.R. ERICSSON AND D.F. HENDRY (2005), "General-to-Specific Modeling: An Overview and Selected Bibliography", Federal Reserve Bank International Finance Discussion Paper No. 838, August.

CHANTASASAWAT, B., K.C. FUNG, H. IIZAKA AND A. SIU (2003), "International Competition for Foreign Direct Investment: The Case of China", Paper presented at the Hitotsubashi Conference on International Trade and FDI, Tokyo.

CHANTASASAWAT, B., K.C. FUNG, H. IIZAKA AND A. SIU (2004), "Foreign Direct Investment in East Asia and Latin America: Is there a People's Republic of China Effect?", ADB Institute Discussion Paper N.º17, Tokyo.

DÍAZ-CASSOU, J., A. GARCÍA-HERRERO AND J.L. MOLINA (2006), "The IMF Catalytic Role in Crisis Resolution and Crisis - Prevention", Documento de Trabajo 0617, Banco de España, Madrid.

EWE GHEE L. (2001), *Determinants of, and the Relation Between, Foreign Direct Investment and Growth: A Summary of the Recent Literature*, IMF Working Paper WP/01/175.

GARCÍA-HERRERO, A. AND J. RUIZ (2004), "How Much do Trade and Financial Linkages Matter for Business Cycle Synchronization?", mimeo, Available at: www.eco.uc3m.es/jruiz/TFSynchronization.pdf.

GREENE, W.H. (2003), *Econometric Analysis*, 5th ed. Prentice-Hall, Upper Saddle River, New Jersey.

HAUSSMANN, R. AND E. FERNANDEZ-ARIAS (2000), "Foreign Direct Investment: Good Cholesterol?". IADB, Research Department Working Paper No. 417. Available at SSRN: http://ssrn.com/abstract=252192

HINES, J.R. (1995), "Forbidden Payment: Foreign Bribery and American Business after 1977", NBER Working Paper 5266.

INTER-AMERICAN DEVELOPMENT BANK (IDB) (2004), "The Emergence of China: Opportunities and Challenges For Latin America And The Caribbean", draft for discussion, October Available at: http://www.iadb.org/

JAUMOTTE, F. (2004), "Foreign Direct Investment and Regional Trade Agreements: The Market Size Effect Revisited", Working Paper Nº 04/206, IMF, Washington, D.C.

LANE, P.R. AND G.M. MILESI-FERRETTI (2004), "Financial Globalization and Exchange Rates", mimeo, IMF, Washington, D.C.

LEVY-YEYATI, E., E. PANIZZA AND U. STEIN (2002), "The Cyclical Nature of North-South FDI Flows", paper presented at the Joint Conference of IDB-WB, The FDI Race: Who Gets the Prize? Is it Worth the Effort?

LOVE, J.H. AND F. LAGEHIDALGO (2000), "Analysing the Determinants of US Direct Investment in Mexico", *Applied Economics*, 32, pp. 1259-1267.

MODY, A., S. DASGUPTA AND S. SINHA (1998), "Japanese Multinationals in Asia: Drivers and Attractors", *Oxford Development Studies*, Vol. 27, Nº 2, pp. 149-164.

MOORE, M.O. (1993), "Determinants of German Manufacturing Direct Investment: 1980-1988", *Weltwirtschaftsliches Archiv*, 129, pp. 120-137.

SINGH, H. AND K. JUN (1995), "Some New Evidence on Determinants of Foreign Direct Investment in Developing Countries", World Bank Policy Research Working Paper Nº 2338, Washington, D.C.

WEI, S. (1997), "Why is Corruption So Much More Taxing Than Taxes? Arbitrariness Kills", National Bureau of Economic Research Working Paper 6255.

OECD PUBLICATIONS, 2, rue André-Pascal, 75775 PARIS CEDEX 16
PRINTED IN FRANCE
(41 2007 03 1 P) ISBN 978-92-64-02796-1 – No. 55579 2007